What People are Saying about Spiritual Gifts for Spiritual Warfare

As soon as I started reading *Spiritual Gifts for Spiritual Warfare*, I felt like a child who has just received a favorite toy for his birthday. It kept me reading, on and on, one chapter after another—nonstop! I was blessed to be enlightened by so many powerful revelations about the gifts of the Holy Spirit. With a great gift for teaching, Tom Brown brings forth wonderful, liberating truths with a unique simplicity, so that anyone reading this book will be able to understand it and to benefit greatly from it. I highly recommend this book to all serious Christians and to anyone who desires to experience the gifts of the Holy Spirit and a life of victory over all the schemes of the enemy!

—Dr. Gordon-John Manchè
Senior Pastor, River of Love Christian Fellowship, Malta (EU)
CEO, Nations for Christ Ministries International
www.nationsforchrist.org

In *Spiritual Gifts for Spiritual Warfare*, Tom Brown presents the Christian church with an important work. This book offers clear, easy to understand, and useable tools to break free, once and for all, from the traps of Satan. He offers real-life examples of people just like you, as well as biblical weapons to help you defeat the enemy. I highly recommend this significant contribution and fresh perspective to the global spiritual warfare library.

—Dr. Steven Swisher
President, Swisher Evangelistic Association, Inc.
Executive Director, Believers Stand United
Senior Pastor, Epiphany United Methodist Church
Cincinnati, Ohio

With tremendous spiritual experience and success, Tom Brown effectively entices readers to plug in to the power of the Holy Spirit in order to get the gifts flowing.

—*Chas Stevenson*
Pastor, Houston Faith Church, Houston, Texas

I have known Tom Brown for many years. I esteem him as a seasoned pastor, a man of God, an anointed teacher, and a good friend. That's why I am recommending his latest book, *Spiritual Gifts for Spiritual Warfare*. I don't just routinely write recommendations for books; I have to like and value what the book is all about. With his writing, Tom gets me thinking and studying God's Word. He has spent considerable time studying and documenting these extremely important subjects, subjects that are often so sadly neglected in many of our modern churches. I particularly like his in-depth treatment of subjects like the baptism in the Holy Spirit and speaking in tongues, and the benefits they bring. This book fills a gap in much of the teaching in today's church, as it brings desperately needed truths on these relevant and important New Testament subjects.

—*Dr. Col Stringer*
President, International Convention of Faith Ministries Australia
Robina, Queensland, Australia

Are spiritual gifts alive in the church today? Tom Brown answers with a resounding "Yes!" in his new book *Spiritual Gifts for Spiritual Warfare*. Unfortunately, some theologians insist that spiritual gifts have ceased in modern times, but this book proves, both biblically and experientially, that the Holy Spirit is active and miraculously moving in the lives of those who believe. If you want to activate spiritual gifts in your life, you need to read this book.

—Daniel King
www.kingministries.com
Tulsa, Oklahoma

Unlike most books on the Holy Spirit, filled with the history of the Holy Spirit, *Spiritual Gifts for Spiritual Warfare* takes you inside the mind of God, like an intriguing Tom Clancy novel. With deft clarity, you will learn, experience, and find new eagerness to walk and operate in the power of the Holy Spirit. This book will encourage newcomers to the faith to learn about the Holy Spirit, and will strengthen those who once walked closely with the Holy Spirit, to do so once again. An honest and accurate page-turner, filled with excellent revelation, this is a book that every Christian should add to his or her personal library.

—David Gonzalez
Pastor, author, televangelist, and theologian
David Gonzalez Ministries
Wisconsin Dells, Wisconsin

SPIRITUAL GIFTS *for* SPIRITUAL WARFARE

TOM BROWN

WHITAKER
HOUSE

Unless otherwise indicated, all Scripture quotations are taken from the *Holy Bible, New International Version*®, NIV®, © 1973, 1978, 1984 by the International Bible Society. Used by permission of Zondervan. All rights reserved. Scripture quotations marked (ASV) are taken from the American Standard Edition of the Revised Version of the Holy Bible. Scripture quotations marked (NKJV) are taken from the *New King James Version*, © 1979, 1980, 1982, 1984 by Thomas Nelson, Inc. Used by permission. All rights reserved. Scripture quotations marked (AMP) are taken from the *Amplified® Bible*, © 1954, 1958, 1962, 1964, 1965, 1987 by The Lockman Foundation. Used by permission. (www.Lockman.org). Scripture quotations marked (NLT) are taken from the *Holy Bible, New Living Translation*, © 1996, 2004, 2007. Used by permission of Tyndale House Publishers, Inc., Carol Stream, Illinois 60188. All rights reserved. Scripture quotations marked (KJV) are taken from the King James Version of the Holy Bible.

Boldface type in the Scripture quotations indicates the author's emphasis.

SPIRITUAL GIFTS FOR SPIRITUAL WARFARE

Tom Brown
P.O. Box 27275
El Paso, TX 79926
www.tbm.org

ISBN: 978-1-62911-279-4
eBook ISBN: 978-1-62911-280-0
Printed in the United States of America
© 2015 by Tom Brown

Whitaker House
1030 Hunt Valley Circle
New Kensington, PA 15068
www.whitakerhouse.com

Library of Congress Cataloging-in-Publication Data

Brown, Tom, 1963-
 Spiritual gifts for spiritual warfare / by Tom Brown.
     pages cm
 Summary: "In Spiritual Gifts for Spiritual Warfare, Tom Brown presents the spiritual gifts given by God and equips readers to use them to overcome temptation and to defeat Satan"— Provided by publisher.
 ISBN 978-1-62911-279-4 (trade pbk. : alk. paper) — ISBN 978-1-62911-280-0 (ebook) 1. Gifts, Spiritual. 2. Spiritual warfare. I. Title.
 BT767.3.B76 2015
 235'.4—dc23
                                                        2014050164

No part of this book may be reproduced or transmitted in any form or by any means, electronic or mechanical—including photocopying, recording, or by any information storage and retrieval system—without permission in writing from the publisher. Please direct your inquiries to permissionseditor@whitakerhouse.com.

CONTENTS

Preface: Satan Fears the Holy Spirit 9
Introduction: Helper 15

Part 1: Baptism in the Holy Spirit

1. The Coming of the Holy Spirit 27
2. You Will Receive Power 33
3. The Day of Pentecost 37
4. The Spirit Comes After Salvation 45
5. Baptism in the Cloud 51
6. The Seal 55
7. Is Tongues the Evidence? 63
8. How to Receive the Holy Spirit 69

Part 2: The Gifts of the Holy Spirit

9. Ignorance and Rejection of the Gifts 77
10. The Bells Are Heard Again 83
11. Gifts Are Supernatural 89
12. Message of Wisdom 95
13. Message of Knowledge 105
14. Special Faith 115
15. Gifts of Healing 123

16. Working of Miracles 131
17. Prophecy 137
18. Discerning of Spirits 149
19. Tongues and Interpretation 157
20. How to Activate the Gifts 167
21. The Fruit of the Spirit 175

Afterword: Have the Gifts Passed Away? 185

About the Author 191

PREFACE

SATAN FEARS THE HOLY SPIRIT

Captain Aaron Johnson[1] drove hundreds of miles to meet me at my church in El Paso, Texas. He was neatly dressed in full army khakis. The cross on his right collar signified that he was a chaplain. He came to see me for guidance and prayer, and he told me a fantastic story.

He grew up in the home of Southern Baptist parents, and although they attended church every Sunday, the reality of Christ and His teachings had not influenced his family. At the age of eight, he found pornography and was soon addicted to it. When he turned sixteen, however, he felt God calling him into the ministry. After high school, he attended a Southern Baptist Seminary and learned good basic theology. For the first time, his eyes were enlightened and he came to the knowledge of salvation. It was in seminary that he was born again and baptized.

Though Aaron had learned about salvation at the school, he knew nothing of the baptism of the Holy Spirit or of real spiritual warfare. Certainly, Satan was mentioned but he had not learned how to use the gifts of the Spirit against his archenemy. In fact, he

---

1. Fictional name

had often heard that certain spiritual gifts were no longer operating in the lives of believers. Additionally, the gifts that *did* exist were often described secularly rather than biblically. He had no practical understanding of spiritual warfare and how the gifts of the Spirit could be used to win battles against Satan.

During his time in seminary, Aaron met his wife. She wanted to be a missionary; they were a good match. They got married a year after Aaron was saved. Eventually, he became a chaplain and fathered two children. Things seemed to be going fine until he was deployed to Afghanistan. It was there that he again became hooked on pornography and his personality began to change.

After Aaron returned home, his wife immediately became aware that her husband had changed for the worse. He experienced frequent bursts of anger and had difficulty controlling his temper. After years of enduring her husband's fits of rage, Aaron's wife lost patience and filed for a divorce.

Alone and bewildered, Aaron seriously considered suicide. Only his fear of God kept him from this selfish and desperate act. Still, he was tortured by his thoughts. Why had he changed so drastically? How could he get rid of his anger and his addiction to pornography? Aaron knew of nothing strong enough to break the bondages of pornography, anger, suicidal thoughts, and his controlling personality.

When none of the Baptist ministers he consulted were able to help him, Aaron turned to a couple of Pentecostal chaplains. Without confessing his addiction, he told the chaplains about his anger, controlling personality, and about his wife filing for divorce. As the Pentecostal chaplains began to pray for him, one of them stated, "You are into pornography and have opened a door for other demons to come into your life. Not only you, but your son also is into pornography. There is a generational curse of pornography in your family."

When Aaron heard this, he recognized the truth. He had not confessed his addiction to pornography that started in his childhood. But God already knew this and had revealed it to the chaplain, not to expose and humiliate Aaron but to free him. Aaron confessed that it was true.

The chaplains begin to pray deliverance over him and, immediately, an evil spirit caused great pain in his stomach. Aaron said it was the worse physical pain he had ever experienced. As soon as the spirit came out of him, the pain stopped; but a second spirit did the same, causing even more pain than the first. Just when he thought he could take no more, a third evil spirit manifested and the pain increased. Soon, a fourth spirit manifested itself and the pain became almost unbearable. Finally, a fifth and final spirit spoke to Aaron in a voice that sounded like a woman, saying, "I am the one in control here. I do not want to go." Nevertheless, it left. Finally, he was completely delivered.

Aaron told me that since his deliverance six months prior, he had not had a desire to look at pornography and his feelings of anger were gone. During the previous week, he had been filled with the Holy Spirit and had spoken in tongues for the first time.

He said, "I have read two of your books on spiritual warfare, and I'm new to all this, but I am convinced that I was truly delivered. I just want to make sure there is no demon remaining in me. I feel a little dazed by all this. Do you think I am free?"

I told him that I did not discern any spirits still within him but that his feelings of confusion may stem more from the aftermath of war. Using his military background to create an analogy, I told him, "The allies drove out the enemy from the city, but the city still has residual damage. The victory did not quickly fix all the damages of the enemy. So it is with you, Aaron. You now must rebuild your life with the Word of God and through the power of the Spirit."

Now that he had personally experienced spiritual warfare, Aaron needed to know the gifts of the Spirit, so that he could use them as weapons against Satan. I encouraged him to use his new knowledge to help others be freed from Satan's power.

That is what this book is about. This book contains what I would have taught Aaron if I'd had the time. It is about your weapons of warfare. In my previous books, I have focused on knowing the enemy, which is essential, since any good soldier must understand his opponent. However, he must also know of all the weapons that are available. In this volume, I will focus on your Friend and Helper, the Holy Spirit, and the weapons He has given you to use against Satan. These weapons are called the gifts of the Spirit.

One thing I have learned over three decades of casting out demons is this: Satan fears the Holy Spirit. The Holy Spirit was everything to Jesus. He said, *"I drive out demons by the Spirit of God"* (Matthew 12:28). Jesus did not drive out demons by virtue of His deity. If He had, there would be no hope for us to drive out Satan from our lives and the lives of our loved ones. Instead, Jesus depended on the power of the Spirit to accomplish His powerful exorcism ministry, and He made this same power available to you. You have the same gifts that Jesus used!

Only the Holy Spirit can drive out demonic spirits. No human power can defeat Satan; since he is a lawless spirit, only the good Spirit can defeat him. You do not need to be totally good to win, but you do need to depend on the virtue of the Holy Spirit to help you. And the Spirit will give you gifts to defeat Satan.

Before I begin teaching about gifts of the Spirit, you must be aware of how Satan will try to defeat you. First, he will try to deceive you. But with the wisdom and knowledge that God gives, you can uncover his deceptions. Second, he will try to discourage you. Satan will throw every test and trial your way to convince you to give up. But through the power of the Spirit, you can overcome every obstacle. Third, he will try to tempt you. He will entice you with various temptations to get you hooked to his bondages. He wants to make you a slave. But through the Holy Spirit working within you, you avoid sin by saying no to temptation.

Another reason I have written this book is to show you that you are not alone. You have a Helper who will help you defeat Satan. Don't be alarmed by the enemy's wiles. No matter what Satan has been bombarding you with, there is a greater Spirit within you.

We know that Satan is *"the ruler of the kingdom of the air, the spirit who is now at work in those who are disobedient"* (Ephesians 2:2). Yet the Holy Spirit is the new Ruler for the Christian soul, and He is the greater Spirit within us that overcomes Satan by working in those who are obedient to Christ. You need to know of all the weapons God has given you to overcome Satan. *"Greater is he that is in you than he that is in the world"* (1 John 4:4 ASV). The first pronoun *"he"* is not a reference to Christ or God the Father; here, John is referring to the Holy Spirit. Many believers know a lot about Christ and their Creator, but they give little thought to the Holy Spirit. This is why so many are defeated.

I hope you prayerfully read this book and allow the Holy Spirit to show you the weapons of your warfare. May God bless you as you embark on the fabulous study of discovering the gifts of the Holy Spirit.

INTRODUCTION

HELPER

And I will pray the Father, and He will give you another **Helper**, *that He may abide with you forever.*
—John 14:16 (NKJV)

"Helper"—this is the perfect job description of the Holy Spirit! He is there to help you. This implies that you *do* need help! We cannot live the kind of life God wants us to live without His divine help.

God did not simply forgive us our sins, write our names in heaven, and then say, "Try your best to live for Me." No! He knows we are incapable of pleasing Him, no matter how hard we try; so He gave us a precious gift: the Holy Spirit. Just as we cannot save ourselves without Christ, we also cannot live a saved life without the Holy Spirit. What I mean by *a saved life* is the life God intends us to live as saved people—dead to sin, alive to God, and victorious in this life. (See Romans 6:11.) God does not want us to continue living as we did before salvation, and salvation alone cannot empower us to live the supernatural life. We need the Holy Spirit.

The Holy Spirit helps us so that we—His children—can live supernaturally. God does not want us to live natural, normal lives. He wants us to live above normal, above the natural. And this is possible through the Holy Spirit.

As a Helper, the Holy Spirit will contribute strength and means, by which we can win battles; He renders us assistance and cooperates effectively with us. He does not work alone but with us.

This is very different from Christ's work of redemption. Christ did not need our help in taking away the sins of the world; He did not need our help in moving the stone away from the tomb at His resurrection; rather, He did it all Himself![2]

Unlike Christ, who alone accomplished redemption for us on the cross and through His resurrection, the Holy Spirit accomplishes His work with us and through us. He never works alone. He joins with us to defeat Satan.

For example, if you need help lifting a couch and a friend comes to assist you, you would not leave the room and wait for him to move the couch alone; rather, you would take one end and your friend would take the other and, together, you would move the couch. This is how the Holy Spirit helps us. He contributes something supernatural to our efforts so that we can accomplish divine work, receive victory, and become the person God intends for us to be. But He won't do this work alone; He needs our cooperation.

This is why we need more teaching on the Holy Spirit. We need to know our role and function in collaboration and cooperation with His work. Many times, the Spirit is hampered by our lack of discernment and cooperation. This book will teach you how to cooperate with the Holy Spirit, so that God's perfect will is accomplished in your life.

Three Areas of Help

There are three primary areas in which the Holy Spirit helps us. These three areas are like trees—they branch out in many

---

2. In Christ's earthly ministry, He helped people through His teachings and miracles. However, in His substitutionary death on the cross, He suffered alone. Man contributed nothing positive to Christ's redemptive death and resurrection.

different directions. Basically, the Holy Spirit makes you smarter, stronger, and better.

He Will Make You Smarter

The Spirit of the Lord *will rest on him—the Spirit of* **wisdom** *and of* **understanding**, *the Spirit of* **counsel** *and of power, the Spirit of* **knowledge** *and of the fear of the* Lord.
(Isaiah 11:2)

Notice the four areas in which the Holy Spirit works: (1) *"wisdom,"* (2) *"understanding,"* (3) *"counsel,"* and (4) *"knowledge."* This is the primary help the Holy Spirit provides. If a person grows in wisdom, he or she will have a more successful marriage and family; a more profitable business, career, and ministry; a better social and civic life; and so much more. Look at the benefits of wisdom: *"Long life is in her right hand; in her left hand are riches and honor"* (Proverbs 3:16). Wisdom carries with her long life, riches, and honor. When you get wisdom, you get the rest. It's like a story of a little boy named Johnny who sits on Santa Claus's lap. Santa asks him the usual question: "Johnny, what would you like for Christmas?" Johnny thinks for a moment about what he wants, then he surprises Santa, saying, "I want, uh, uh…I want *you*, Santa." The boy realized that if he gets Santa, he inherits the North Pole and all the elves that work for him. He knows that Santa has all the gifts. If he gets the giver of the gifts, he gets *all* the gifts.

This is wisdom. When you get wisdom, along with it, you get long life, wealth, and honor. Solomon even said that wisdom *"yields better returns than gold"* (Proverbs 3:14). Many people are looking for high returns on their investments. Well, wisdom gives the best returns, interest, and dividends.

Where do we get this true wisdom? Human intelligence is part of it; but alone, it cannot help us make wise choices. This is where the Holy Spirit comes in. He gives us a wisdom that we were not given at birth. He makes us smarter than we are naturally. He provides us with additional brain power.

People have commented on how smart I am. Someone will say, "I bet you were in the top ten percent of your class." The truth is, I was in the part of the class that made the top ten percent possible. There was nothing exceptional about me in school. Yet God has given me supernatural wisdom that has enabled me to build a large church, negotiate business deals, write books, be my own webmaster of a huge Internet site, and produce television programs aired on top networks. Furthermore, God gave me the honor of leading a successful initiative in my city to push back a radical gay agenda. I could accomplish this only with the *"favor with God and men"* (Luke 2:52). Catholics, Protestants, and Mormons worked with me to pass the ordinance. Why would these religious groups want to work with a crazy charismatic like myself? Wisdom. God-given wisdom enabled me to go beyond my human intelligence and gain favor within my community. This wisdom is not something one can boast in, because it comes from God.

Solomon also understood the source of his wisdom. When two women claimed to be the mother of his child, he, without the help of DNA samples, was skillful in what he decided. Knowing the true mother would do anything to save her child, Solomon said, *"Cut the living child in two and give half to one [mother] and half to the other"* (1 Kings 3:25). Immediately the true mother said, *"Please, my lord, give her the living baby! Don't kill him!"* (verse 26). The other woman thought that this was a fair proposal. (See verse 26.) Solomon, in that instant, knew who the mother was, and he gave the baby to the woman who was willing to lose the child in order to save its life. *"When all Israel heard the verdict the king had given, they held the king in awe, because they saw that he had wisdom from God to administer justice"* (1 Kings 3:28). The people recognized the true source of Solomon's wisdom—*"wisdom from God"* (verse 28).

Solomon was born no smarter a person than the average man, but when he prayed and asked for wisdom, he received supernatural wisdom to exceptionally govern God's people.

How about you? Do you think you would benefit from God-given wisdom? Of course you would! And I will try to help you understand how to receive the wisdom that the Holy Spirit wants to impart to you.

He Will Make You Stronger

Isaiah called this ability the *"Spirit of...power"* (Isaiah 11:2). Power is the Word of God. Power is supernatural ability. You need this ability to share the Word, to be a good spouse, to love your enemies, to be victorious, and to do anything God calls you to do. The good news is that you do not have to rely on your strength to do this. The Holy Spirit has come to empower you to be stronger than you can imagine.

We all have natural abilities, but those abilities can take us only so far; when we have the Holy Spirit, we have greater and even supernatural abilities. We will need these supernatural abilities to overcome our supernatural enemy—Satan. Our natural strength will be no match for Satan's supernatural power, so the Holy Spirit gives us supernatural power over Satan's power.

In *Raiders of the Lost Ark*, the hero, Indiana Jones, was confronted with an enemy skilled in the use of a huge machete. The enemy smirked as he showed his precision with the weapon. Even though Indiana Jones also had a machete, it was clear that he was outmatched by his opponent. Then Indiana Jones smiled. Why wasn't he worried? To everyone's surprise, Indiana Jones pulled out a revolver and shot the enemy. In that scenario, a gun trumps a machete.

We can relate this to spiritual warfare. The devil has power and we have power. But he is much stronger and skilled at using his power than we are, in the natural. But when God gives us spiritual weapons that trump Satan's weapons, we can defeat him, once and for all!

Let me give you an example in the Bible. Samson was an Israelite. There are pictures that depict him as a bodybuilder. Still, no bodybuilder can tear apart a lion with his bare hands. How was he able to do this? *"The Spirit of the LORD came upon him in power so that he tore the lion apart with his bare hands as he might have torn a young goat"* (Judges 14:6). Samson's big muscles did not account for his supernatural feat of tearing apart a lion with his bare hands. The Bible says he was able to do this because *"the Spirit of the LORD came upon him in power."* Without the Spirit, you still have strength to do certain things; however, *with* the Holy Spirit, you can do supernatural things!

One of the most exciting and beneficial spiritual gift is the gift of healing.

> *Now to each one the manifestation of the Spirit is given for the common good. To one there is given through the Spirit the message of wisdom, to another the message of knowledge by means of the same Spirit, to another faith by the same Spirit, to another gifts of healing by that one Spirit.*
>
> (1 Corinthians 12:7–9)

The first two gifts—wisdom and knowledge—are primary. They relate to what we discussed previously about making you smarter. However, the fourth gift on the list is the gift of healing. Now, no human has the ability to heal another person. But with the power of the Holy Spirit, you, like Samson, can do something extraordinary—heal others!

I can vouch for the healing gift in my life. I have seen scores of people healed simply through my touch and simple prayer. Some look at me and others with this gift as though we are out of touch with reality. They scoff at the thought of someone healing another through the laying on of hands. I understand people's skepticism, because, in the natural, no one has this power. But the Holy Spirit has come to impart this gift to God's people.

People will come to me and say, "C'mon, Bishop. Be honest. You have never really seen anyone healed through your prayers." But I can honestly say that yes, I have.

One Sunday in particular stands out in my memory. An injured police officer came up to me with his walker. I laid hands on him and spoke a word of faith—"You can walk in Jesus' name." Then he handed me the walker and started to walk on his own. I am not a skeptic, but I marvel at the power of God. The people in church were jumping up and down as they saw this miracle with their own eyes. The officer was weeping with joy as he was truly healed.

The next person in line was on crutches. I laid hands on him, and said, "Well, you saw what God did with the first man. How about you? Do you think you need the crutches?" Joyfully and without hesitation, he handed me the crutches and walked and ran without any sign of injury. The congregation was beside themselves with joy as they saw two miracles, one after the other.

I am an eyewitness of these two healings. It is one thing to argue about one person walking without crutches or a walker, but two miracles, back-to-back? I will be the first to tell you that I cannot heal anyone in my own power. Thankfully, I am not living in my own power but in the power of the Holy Spirit.

In this book, I want you to discover the gifts the Holy Spirit wants to give you, and I will teach you how to pray for, expect, and activate those gifts.

He Will Make You Better

Do you desire to be a better person? Would you like to be more loving and caring for others? How about being patient and kind? Maybe you just want to be a good person. Well, this is what the Holy Spirit will do for you. He will make you a better person. You will be more excellent, more suitable, and more favorable, surpassing your past character. The Holy Spirit will make you into an improved you. He improves your life. The Bible calls this improvement "holiness." The Spirit is called holy for a reason. Holiness is the opposite of sin. When the Spirit comes into a person's life, He makes him or her holy. Isaiah called Him the *"Spirit of the…fear of the* Lord*"* (Isaiah 11:2). Fear of the Lord inspires us to live holy lives.

Every saved Christian struggles with sin, be they addictions, habits, or compulsions. Many Christians struggle with gluttony, alcohol, pornography, anger, jealousy, greed, and other vices. These sins are difficult to remove from a person's life, and many wonder if and when they will be able to overcome these depravities. On your own, you can't, but, with the sanctifying work of the Spirit, you can.

After suffering from a hangover, former President George W. Bush quit drinking—cold turkey. Despite being a heavy drinker throughout most of his life, he put an abrupt end to his drinking days. How was this possible? Bush credits God in giving him the strength to overcome his drinking problem. It was the Holy Spirit within George Bush's life that sanctified him from his unhealthy habit.

Experts insist that recovering alcoholics need therapy. While I am happy for those who have stopped drinking through the help of therapy, there is another Helper who can make people stop drinking. He is the Holy Spirit and He gives us the power to live holy.

Alcoholics Anonymous encourages recovering alcoholics to admit that they are powerless to stop drinking on their own. It teaches them to focus on a "higher power." Well, the higher power has a name: the Holy Spirit. When you focus on His power, you discover that you have more strength than you had on your own. The Holy Spirit will help you to live a better life.

What This Book Will Do for You

It is my intention to help you yield to the Holy Spirit, so that you can live the full life in the Spirit. The first thing this book will show you is the importance of experiencing baptism in the Holy Spirit. Without this Spirit baptism, you will be limited as to how much the Holy Spirit can help you. Second, it will teach you how to receive the Holy Spirit in your life. Third, this book will point out the various ways in which the Holy Spirit can work in your life. Fourth, this volume will teach you how to recognize and activate the various gifts in your life.

How This Book Is Arranged

This book is divided into two sections. The first section deals with the importance of the baptism in the Spirit and why a Christian must experience it after his or her conversion. Without receiving the baptism in the Spirit, you will not be given the full range of the gifts of the Spirit. Thus, I have devoted an entire section to Spirit baptism, in order to help you understand the importance of this gift.

The second section discusses the nine gifts of the Spirit mentioned in 1 Corinthians 12. The book concludes with a section on the fruits of the Spirit, which must accompany the gifts.

Get ready to experience the move of the Holy Spirit.

PART 1

BAPTISM IN THE HOLY SPIRIT

ONE

THE COMING OF THE HOLY SPIRIT

When the day of Pentecost came, they were all together in one place. Suddenly a sound like the blowing of a violent wind came from heaven and filled the whole house where they were sitting. They saw what seemed to be tongues of fire that separated and came to rest on each of them. All of them were filled with the Holy Spirit and began to speak in other tongues as the Spirit enabled them.
—Acts 2:1–4

The greatest event in human history is not the birth of Christ or His death or His resurrection—the greatest event in history is Pentecost. Oh, I am not downplaying the work of Christ, because without His work, the Holy Spirit could not come. My point is that the work of Christ was intended to make possible the work of the Holy Spirit. After Christ accomplished everything He was sent to do, God sent the Spirit. *"Up to that time the Spirit had not been given, since Jesus had not yet been glorified"* (John 7:39).

God brought redemption through His Son so that He could bring power to His children. If redemption itself were the sole purpose of God's plan, then we would simply be forgiven sinners still bound by sin. We would simply be normal, forgiven people. But God's intent was to radically change us, and He does this in our lives through the work of the Spirit. With the Holy Spirit, and His gifts at work in our lives, we can live in the supernatural. Satan lives in the supernatural, so we need the supernatural gift of the Holy Spirit to live as God wants us to live—overcoming sin!

The Forgotten God

Francis Chan calls the Holy Spirit "the forgotten God." Maybe this is too strong of a statement, but he makes a great point. Too often, the church knows much about God and His Son Jesus, but little thought is given to the third person of the Trinity. He is nearly forgotten.

It is not just the contemporary church that neglects the Holy Spirit, but past tradition also shows a real neglect of the Holy Spirit. For example, in the famous Apostles' Creed, much attention is given to God the Creator and even more attention to the Son, yet the creed lends only a few short words to the Spirit: *"Credo in Spiritum Sanctum,"* or "I believe in the Holy Spirit," and *"Dominum nostrum, qui conceptus est de Spiritu Sancto,"* or "Our Lord, who was conceived by the Holy Spirit." There is no explanation of His work or ministry, or who or what He is.

It is not just our apostolic fathers who neglected the Holy Spirit but also the church in general throughout the history of Christendom. Consider the Christian holidays. Everyone makes a big deal about celebrating Christ's birth at Christmas, and rightly so. Then there is Good Friday and Easter, during which we celebrate His sacrifice and our redemption. Churches are packed during these holidays. But fifty days later, few Christians give any special thoughts about Pentecost Sunday. Pentecost, unfortunately, has become the stepchild of Christian holidays. We know it's there but we pay it little attention. No wonder the church seems powerless. Pentecost is the coming of the Holy Spirit into the world in the same sense that Christ came into the world. God the Father, Christ the Son, and the Spirit have always existed. The Spirit was present and active in the lives of Old Testament saints but He was limited in His work. Pentecost marks the beginning of His full ministry.

Pentecost should carry the same weight as other Christian holidays among Christians. It should be recognized and celebrated with gift giving, because the Spirit also gives gifts. Without Pentecost, Christmas, Easter, the incarnation, and the resurrection all lose their true meaning and significance.

The Missing Ingredient

I invented a delicious tortilla soup recipe. It was ranked the number one tortilla soup on Google for seven years straight. It has since been surpassed by other soup recipes but, in my humble opinion, it is still the best recipe. Many have made my soup. When my mother tried making it for the first time, she called me, and said, "Tom, something is wrong with the soup. It doesn't taste like yours."

"Well, you are missing an ingredient," I said. "Let's go over it again. You put in the tomatoes and cilantro, right?"

"Yes."

"Did you remember the chipotle peppers?"

"Of course, I remembered those. That's the secret to the recipe."

"Well," I continued, "I assume you put in the onions?"

My mom squealed. "Oh! I can't believe I forgot the onions! That is one of the main ingredients."

She forgot one of the obvious ingredients, making her soup taste bad. This is what has happened to many Christians. They look somewhat like Christ, but they know something is missing in their lives. And I can tell you that the missing ingredient is the Holy Spirit. Oh, many people acknowledge His existence, but they have never had Him truly enter their lives in a dramatic fashion as we have seen on the day of Pentecost.

My Experience

I grew up in an Assemblies of God church, which is the largest Pentecostal denomination. You would have assumed that I was really acquainted with the power of the Holy Spirit, but I was not. Oh, I heard speaking in tongues and saw some ministers pray for the sick, but I never experienced the Holy Spirit.

It wasn't until I was a senior in high school that I first experienced Him. I attended a Sunday night service at the church when the senior pastor was out of town. The associate pastor took his place behind the pulpit and taught about Peter walking on the water. He told us that with the Holy Spirit, you can do what is humanly impossible, which is what every minister needs. Ministers of the gospel cannot fulfill the call of God unless they receive the Holy Spirit. Just then, he paused. The expression on his face was a bit distant but attentive. God was speaking to him. Then he spoke: "God has shown me that there are two young men in this service that He has called into the ministry. And you two need to come forward and commit your lives to the ministry. God will give you the power you need to be successful."

The first man who went forward was a tall, slender man named Timmy. I thought to myself, *Yes, Timmy will make a good minister.* After he went forward, no one else walked down the aisle. The minister would not accept this. He said, "Look, God is never wrong. He told me that there are two men, not one, whom He has called into the ministry. Hurry, come forward."

Still, no one went forward. I thought, *Who is rebelling by not going forward?* Just then, the minister said, "I knew it was you."

Then he pointed to me. Why would he assume it was me? As I looked around, I noticed that I had stood up. I don't remember standing; it was an unconscious response. Then I walked forward, still bewildered at what had happened.

As I stood next to Timmy, I scanned the front of the church. To my left, I saw Mrs. Hageman, the senior pastor's wife, playing the organ. While looking at her, I felt a gush of love and power flowing in me. Suddenly I fell to the ground and started sobbing uncontrollably. There on the floor, my face to the ground, I continued to pour out my tears on the red carpet. I am sure many people before me had stained the old carpet with tears; but for the first time, I was one of the sincere believers who had received a touch from God.

I was unaware of the time but later found out that I was on the floor for more than an hour. As I neared the end of my weeping, I plainly heard this Scripture in my head: *"And they were all filled with the Holy Ghost, and began to speak with other tongues, as the Spirit gave them utterance"* (Acts 2:4 KJV). At that point, I realized that I was experiencing the baptism in the Spirit that Jesus had told His disciples about: *"Do not leave Jerusalem, but wait for the gift my Father promised, which you have heard me speak about. For John baptized with water, but in a few days you will be baptized with the Holy Spirit"* (Acts 1:4–5). This was it! I had experienced the baptism in the Holy Spirit. Then the thought occurred to me that the proof I had of the Holy Spirit was not tears but speaking tongues. And with that simple revelation, I opened my mouth and spoke in tongues for the first time. It was simple. The language was not from my mind but from the Holy Spirit within me.

After praying in tongues for quite some time, I heard Timmy's voice—"Hey, Tom!"

Not realizing that Timmy had experienced what I had experienced, I turned my face to my right as my body still hugged the carpet. Surprised that Timmy was on the floor with me, I replied, "Yea, Timmy?"

He said, "I can't get off the floor. I'm stuck. I'm just curious, can you get off the floor?"

I hadn't tried before then. I had been so caught up in what God was doing. So I tried to get up but couldn't. "No, Timmy. I can't get up. I feel like I am glued to the floor."

"Me, too. I just thought I was crazy; now I know it has happened to you, too."

So Timmy and I quietly rested while the Spirit of God worked in our lives. Before long, Timmy and I were released from the floor at the same time.

I cannot explain to you everything that happened to me that night. But I believe that as I committed my life to the ministry, God gave me my own Pentecost experience. Just as it happened with the early disciples, I, too, was filled with the Spirit. I believe this experience has given me supernatural abilities that I needed in order to pastor a successful church, write books, preach powerfully, heal the sick, and cast out demons. And you need this experience, too.

TWO

YOU WILL RECEIVE POWER

> *But you will receive power when the Holy Spirit comes on you; and you will be my witnesses in Jerusalem, and in all Judea and Samaria, and to the ends of the earth.*
> —Acts 1:8

Power makes all the difference in a person's life. In this passage, the word *"power"* comes from the Greek word *dunamis*, which is the word for *dynamite*, an explosive power. One of the signs of the baptism in the Holy Spirit is explosive power. This is not ordinary human power but supernatural power. Just as no human has the power to blow up a building (for that, he needs dynamite), so, too, we need the dynamite of the Holy Spirit to blow up the works of the devil. Power means ability. When you are given power, you are given abilities that you do not normally possess.

Jesus did not perform any miracles until He received the Holy Spirit at His baptism. *"And the Holy Spirit descended on him in bodily form like a dove"* (Luke 3:22). After this, He was able to conquer temptation and testing. *"Jesus returned to Galilee in the power of the Spirit, and news about him spread through the whole countryside. He taught in their synagogues, and everyone praised him"* (Luke 4:14–15). Now Jesus was walking in *"the power of the Spirit,"* and with this newfound power, He began His ministry. The Scripture passage describing the launching of His ministry was about the Holy Spirit:

> The scroll of the prophet Isaiah was handed to him. Unrolling it, he found the place where it is written: "The Spirit of the Lord is on me, because he has anointed me to preach good news to the poor. He has sent me to proclaim freedom for the prisoners and recovery of sight for the blind, to release the oppressed, to proclaim the year of the Lord's favor."
>
> (Luke 4:17–19)

Jesus declared what the Holy Spirit would enable Him to do: first, He was enabled to *"preach good news."* Some people are naturally good at speaking; others are not. However, the first ability the Spirit gives us is the power to preach and teach. Second, He was given the power to deliver and heal the oppressed and sick.

Jesus' healing and deliverance ministry was empowered by the Holy Spirit. Prior to receiving the Spirit, Jesus could not perform His designated ministry. It is hard to comprehend that without the Spirit, Jesus could not heal the sick or cast out demons. But according to Scriptures, Jesus' first miracle was turning water into wine, which occurred after He had received the Holy Spirit. *"This, the first of his miraculous signs, Jesus performed at Cana in Galilee"* (John 2:11; see also John 1:32). This was Jesus' first miracle; He did not perform any miracles until after He had received the Holy Spirit.

Jesus confirmed that this was the reason: *"I tell you the truth, the Son can do nothing by himself"* (John 5:19). Jesus did not, by virtue of being *"the Son,"* have divine ability to do any miracles. Concerning casting out demons, Jesus said, *"I drive out demons by the Spirit of God"* (Matthew 12:28). The Holy Spirit gave Jesus power to cast out demons. Peter commented on Jesus' healing ministry, *"God anointed Jesus of Nazareth with the Holy Spirit and power, and how he went around doing good and healing all who were under the power of the devil"* (Acts 10:38). Jesus' power to heal came from the Holy Spirit.

Just as Jesus did not have natural ability to perform miraculous powers by virtue of sonship, so too, Christians lack the ability to perform miraculous powers by virtue of their sonship. Christians must receive the Holy Spirit, and when they do, they will have *"power"* to heal, cast out demons, or perform any other miracles.

Power to Heal

As I mentioned earlier, before I received the baptism in the Spirit, I had not been living holy before the Lord—I'd performed no miracles, healed no one of sickness, or cast out zero demons. I hadn't done anything supernatural!

Soon, I discovered this ability to heal. I read in the Scriptures of Jesus telling us to lay hands on the sick and they would recover (see Mark 16:18), so I gave it a try. My relatives told me that my second cousin Juan had gone blind and was dying in the hospital, so I visited him. I explained to him how I had become a Christian and that the Holy Spirit was in me and wanted to help him recover. I asked him if he wanted me to pray, and he said yes.

I got on my knees, took my cousin by the hand, and began to pray. Suddenly I felt a strange power leaving my hands and going into my cousin. I had never felt this before; it was all new, and I could not explain it. It felt similar to the sensation you feel when your hand falls asleep. After I finished praying, the feeling left me.

My relatives told me about my cousin. They asked, "Did you hear what happened to Juan? He regained his sight and left the hospital." A miracle had taken place. I believe that my prayer had something to do with his miraculous recovery.

I am amazed at how some Christians are skeptical of the power to heal. The trouble is that they forget, or have never realized, that we are not dealing with human power; we are dealing with divine power. No human has this power on his or her own; it is the Holy Spirit who gives us this power.

Casting Out Demons

I can verify that, as it was with Christ, *"I drive out demons by the Spirit of God."* (Matthew 12:28). Three major television networks have featured my deliverance ministry. Four other television producers have asked me about hosting my own television show on exorcism. Doubtless, all this interest proves that something supernatural is taking place. I testify that I have seen numerous people set free from the power of demons.

The first demon I remember dealing with was at a local Bible study in my hometown. I heard a commotion, and I, along with others, went to the room where a woman was lying on her back and screaming. Others began to pray for her, but she continued to scream obscenities at the group. I just watched and silently prayed as others did the work. Finally, the leader turned toward me, and said, "Tom, come and help us pray." I joined the group, ordering the evil spirit to leave the woman. It took about thirty minutes before she was finally freed. After this incident, I realized how real the devil was and how desperately we needed the ministry of deliverance. Yes, through the power of the Spirit, we have power to cast out demons.

THREE

THE DAY OF PENTECOST

> *When **the day of Pentecost** came....[The disciples] were filled with the Holy Spirit and began to speak in other tongues as the Spirit enabled them.*
> —Acts 2:1, 4

Why did God choose this particular day to send His Spirit? To understand why He chose this day, we need to understand its significance. Pentecost actually occurred on the same day as an Old Testament celebration called the Feast of Weeks. Here is the passage in the Old Testament where it is mentioned:

> *From the day after the Sabbath, the day you brought the sheaf of the wave offering, count off seven full weeks. Count off fifty days up to the day after the seventh Sabbath, and then present an offering of new grain to the* LORD. (Leviticus 23:15–16)

This celebrations is called the Feast of Weeks because it occurs *"seven full weeks,"* or fifty days (Pentecost means "fifty"), from the Feast of Firstfruits. We first read about the Feast of Firstfruits here:

> *The* LORD *said to Moses, "Speak to the Israelites and say to them: 'When you enter the land I am going to give you and you reap its harvest, bring to the priest a sheaf of the first grain*

you harvest. He is to wave the sheaf before the LORD so it will be accepted on your behalf; the priest is to wave it on the day after the Sabbath.'"   (Leviticus 23:9–11)

The Feast of Firstfruits occurs on Sunday, the day after the Saturday Sabbath. Since Pentecost is seven weeks from the Feast of Firstfruits, Pentecost also falls on a Sunday. These are the only two biblical feasts established on Sunday—a very important day for Christians. It is the day of the week we celebrate Jesus' resurrection, as well as the day of Pentecost. These events are related to each other, which we will see in a moment.

The Feast of Firstfruits

First, let us look at how the Bible uses the Feast of Firstfruits as a symbol of the resurrection, and then we will see how Pentecost is a symbol of the Holy Spirit. The apostle Paul connects the Feast of Firstfruits with the resurrection of Christ: *"But Christ has indeed been raised from the dead, the firstfruits of those who have fallen asleep"* (1 Corinthians 15:20). The *"firstfruits"* is a symbol of Jesus' resurrection; and since He was resurrected, we, too, shall resurrect. *"Firstfruits"* also suggests our resurrection. The first resurrection of the believer is his spiritual resurrection from death. So Christ's resurrection can bring us resurrection from spiritual death. The Bible calls this spiritual resurrection being "born again." (See, for example, 1 John 1:23.)

Let us look at how James ties together the Feast of Firstfruits with our born-again experience: *"He chose to give us birth through the word of truth, that we might be a kind of firstfruits of all he created"* (James 1:18). We are given this new *"birth through the word of truth, that we might be a kind of firstfruits."* The Feast of Firstfruits symbolizes our spiritual rebirth, our being made alive with Christ in His resurrection.

Notice what the priest did with the firstfruits. After he "reaped the harvest" of the land, he took the grain and waved it on Sunday, the Feast of Firstfruits. The grain offering is the spiritual harvest, or salvation, of souls. Jesus said, *"I tell you, open your eyes and look at the fields! They are ripe for harvest"* (John 4:35). It is clear that we become part of the grain harvest when we are born again. We are the harvest of souls, the sheaves of grain, that Christ, our High Priest, waves before God. Hallelujah!

The Day of Pentecost

Now we come to a very interesting part. How is Pentecost related to the Feast of Firstfruits? After waving the grain offering at the Feast of Firstfruits, the priest would grind the sheaves of grain into flour, then he would add water, oil, and yeast. Next, he would knead the mixture into dough, which was baked into two loaves. On Pentecost, the priest waved the bread before the Lord, as he had done with the sheaves of grain. But this time, the sheaves were turned into edible food. No one eats sheaves; they were meant to be ground and made into bread. So on Pentecost, the once inedible sheaves were made into edible bread and waved before the Lord.

Sheaves or Bread?

This is the difference between being born again and being Spirit-filled. The first offering of the sheaves of grain is a symbol of being born again, while the second offering of bread is a symbol of being filled with the Holy Spirit. What would you rather be a sheaf of grain or bread? This is the difference the Holy Spirit makes in a believer.

This is why Jesus commanded His disciples not to preach until Pentecost: *"On one occasion, while he was eating with them, he gave them this command: 'Do not leave Jerusalem, but wait for the gift my Father promised'"* (Acts 1:4). They were not to leave Jerusalem to evangelize until after the Holy Spirit came. The reason for this is simple: the disciples were inedible sheaves, not prepared and fit to feed anyone the Word of God. It wasn't until the Holy Spirit came on Pentecost that they were filled and ready to make converts. They had been made into bread on Pentecost.

The Feasts of Firstfruits teaches us an important lesson. It is possible to be born again and still have not yet experienced Pentecost. They are different feasts separated by seven weeks. Clearly, being born again is not the same experience as being filled with the Spirit. They are related since they both occur on Sunday and they both require the same grain offering, but they are not the same. But the Feast of Firstfruits must come first; you cannot become bread without first being harvested as grain. In other words, you must first be born again before you can be filled with the Holy Spirit.

This is what the Holy Spirit can do in your life. He can transform you into bread. He can use you to feed the Word to others. Without His power, you will only be able to impart a stale or dry Word that will not ultimately transform others. Or, worse, the devil will trick you into deceiving others through your attempt to teach the Bible. There are false Christian teachers and churches that claim to preach the Word, but since they are not filled with the Spirit, they are easily deceived.

The Oven

An interesting phenomenon took place on the day of Pentecost in the upper room: "[The disciples] *saw what seemed to be tongues of fire that separated and came to rest on each of them*" (Acts 2:3). The fire is symbolic of the oven the priest used to bake the loaves. The imagery of fire is God's way of reminding us that the disciples were being transformed in the fire, or being made ready to preach the Word with their mouths; thus the phrase *"tongues of fire.*" Likewise, your tongue will be touched supernaturally by the Holy Spirit.

Peter's first sermon after Pentecost was powerful. The Bible says that *"when the people heard [it], they were cut to the heart and said to Peter and the other apostles, 'Brothers, what shall we do?'"* (Acts 2:37). His words were so filled with the Holy Spirit that more than three thousand people came to Christ in one day. Peter never had this kind of success before this indwelling of the Holy Spirit.

Yes, Peter did fine sharing the gospel before Pentecost, but he was more effective after Pentecost. Some people may say, "Bishop, I hear what you are saying, but I know some ministers who are good Bible teachers, and they have not experienced the baptism in the Spirit. How do you explain this?"

It's simple; the Holy Spirit is with them helping them do their best. But Pentecost means more than the Holy Spirit being *with* them; Pentecost means the Holy Spirit *in* them. Jesus said, *"The world cannot accept [the Holy Spirit], because it neither sees him nor knows him. But you know him, for he lives with you and will be in you"* (John 14:17). Even before Pentecost, the disciples "knew" the Holy Spirit, because He was always "with them." There is no doubt that the Holy Spirit is with born-again believers and that they *"know him,"* but they can have a much deeper communion with Him when He abides within them. This happens with the Pentecostal experience.

If you are good at teaching the Word without the Pentecostal experience, imagine how much better you will be with it! Don't settle for doing well in your natural ability. Look for something deeper with God. Receive the mighty Pentecostal experience.

First Sheaves, Then Bread

But before you can receive the Pentecostal experience, you have to make sure you are qualified to receive the Holy Spirit.

The Pentecostal bread was *"a wave offering of firstfruits"* (Leviticus 23:17), which means that only those who are *"firstfruits"* can be part of Pentecost. This is confirmed by our Lord when He said that the world could not accept the Holy Spirit. (See John 14:16–17.) The Holy Spirit is not God's gift to the world; God's gift to the world is Jesus: *"For God so loved the world that he gave his one and only Son, that whoever believes in him shall not perish but have eternal life"* (John 3:16).

Jesus is not the same person as the Holy Spirit. He is the second person of the Trinity and is God's gift to the world, so that all can be saved. Jesus is the firstfruits of those who wish to be born again. The Holy Spirit, however, is God's gift to the child of God. Only those who are born again can receive the Holy Spirit; and God's purpose for sending the Spirit is not to save us but to help us live a saved and holy life.

While teaching the principle of asking and receiving, Jesus encouraged the disciples to ask for the Holy Spirit: *"If you then, though you are evil, know how to give good gifts to your children, how much more will your Father in heaven give the Holy Spirit to those who ask him!"* (Luke 11:13). The only people who can ask God to give them the Holy Spirit are those who can call God *"Father."* In other words, you have to be born again before you can ask and expect to receive the Holy Spirit. Only the firstfruits sheaves can become the Pentecost bread.

Have you accepted Christ as your Lord and Savior? All this talk about the Holy Spirit and Pentecost will mean nothing to you unless you are born again. You must first become a sheaf before you can become bread. I invite you to pray this prayer:

Dear God, I come to You in the name of Jesus. I confess that I am a sinner and have disobeyed you from birth. I am deeply sorry for my sinful life, and I repent. Please forgive me. I believe that Jesus was born of the Virgin Mary and that He died for my sins and rose from the dead. I ask You to come inside my heart and to live in me. I believe Christ has saved me. I am born again.

If you have prayed this prayer, you are saved. Now God will give you a better understanding of the kind of bread that God uses to change the world.

What Kind of Bread?

*From wherever you live, bring two loaves made of two-tenths of an ephah of fine flour, baked with yeast, as a wave offering of firstfruits to the L*ORD*.* (Leviticus 23:17)

It is noteworthy that the bread is made with yeast. Yeast symbolizes sin. God is showing that a born-again person does not need to be sinless to be full of the Spirit; in fact, the Holy Spirit helps us conquer sin—the yeast in our lives.

A man once told me that his pastor insisted that if his congregation wanted to be filled with the Spirit, they first must work at getting rid of the sin in their lives, only then would they be able to receive the Spirit. I told the man that his pastor was wrong. I said, "Brother, if you could get rid of the sin without the Holy Spirit, why would you need Him?" He could not answer me.

The bread on Pentecost was made with yeast. Don't let the fact that you have sin in your life keep you from asking God to fill you with the Holy Spirit. Ask God the Father for the Holy Spirit. Let Him fill you with the Holy Spirit. He will help you overcome the effects of sin in your life.

Just as Pentecost was celebrated on the fiftieth day after the Sabbath Passover, so God had another celebration on the fiftieth year—the Year of Jubilee, when everyone's debts were cancelled and the people were freed.

This is what the Holy Spirit intends to do for you; He will make you free when you receive Him into your life. You will be freed from condemnation, from the power of sin, from all diseases, and from Satan's power. The Holy Spirit will liberate you from all the debt and pain you have accumulated during your years as an unbeliever. Satan may have worked for years to bind and enslave you, but the Spirit is the One whom God has sent to free you from all bondages. No longer will you be indebted to the world and to the devil. The Spirit within you will free you!

FOUR

THE SPIRIT COMES AFTER SALVATION

Some people argue with me and insist that when you receive Christ, you automatically receive the Holy Spirit. I totally disagree. The Spirit comes after salvation. Yet Satan has tried to keep believers from seeking the Holy Spirit with this lie, because he is afraid of what will happen if they receive the Spirit. Let us look carefully at what the Word of God says.

Baptism in Water and Baptism in the Holy Spirit

Disciples in Ephesus

While Apollos was at Corinth, Paul took the road through the interior and arrived at Ephesus. There he found some disciples and asked them, "Did you receive the Holy Spirit when you believed?" They answered, "No, we have not even heard that there is a Holy Spirit." So Paul asked, "Then what baptism did you receive?" "John's baptism," they replied. Paul said, "John's baptism was a baptism of repentance. He told the people to believe in the one coming after him, that is, in Jesus." On hearing this, they were baptized into the name of the Lord Jesus.

> When Paul placed his hands on them, the Holy Spirit came on them, and they spoke in tongues and prophesied. There were about twelve men in all. (Acts 19:1–7)

Paul assumed the disciples were believers in Jesus, yet he noticed something lacking in their lives. So the first thing he asked was, "*Did you receive the Holy Spirit when you believed?*" This verse could be translated "Did you receive the Holy Spirit *after* you believed?" Indeed, it is possible to be saved but still not have the Holy Spirit. The question Paul asks these disciples proves that he did not think belief in Jesus automatically meant a Christian was filled with the Holy Spirit.

Today, numerous unbelievers are led in the sinner's prayer and are baptized in water, but little to no thought is given to ensuring that they receive the Holy Spirit. Thus, there are many converts missing out on the baptism in the Holy Spirit. We must give careful thought to our methods of evangelism. It is not enough to teach Sunday school lessons and baptize new believers in water. They must be taught about the baptism in the Holy Spirit and the Spirit-filled life.

> On hearing this, they were baptized into the name of the Lord Jesus. When Paul placed his hands on them, the Holy Spirit came on them, and they spoke in tongues and prophesied. (Acts 19:5–6)

Not only did Paul query whether or not they had received the Spirit, but after they had been water baptized, he laid hands on them so they could receive the Holy Spirit. If water baptism were the end of our salvation experience, why would Paul place his hands on them to impart the Holy Spirit? There are two separate experiences described here: water baptism and Spirit baptism.

New Converts in Samaria

This is not an isolated incident. Consider the new converts in Samaria. They received Christ and were water baptized: *"But when they believed Philip as he preached the good news of the kingdom of God and the name of Jesus Christ, they were baptized, both men and women"* (Acts 8:12). What did they have to do to be saved? Believe the gospel and the name of Jesus Christ. *"Everyone who calls on the name of the Lord will be saved"* (Romans 10:13). In addition to believing in Jesus, they also were baptized in water. This proves that they were saved, for Jesus said, *"Whoever believes and is baptized will be saved"* (Mark 16:16). The Nicene Creed reads, "We acknowledge one baptism for the remission of sins." Their sins were remitted; they were saved in every sense of the word.

However, they did not receive the Holy Spirit:

> *When the apostles in Jerusalem heard that Samaria had accepted the word of God, they sent Peter and John to them. When they arrived, they prayed for them that they might receive the Holy Spirit, because the Holy Spirit had not yet come upon any of them; they had simply been baptized into the name of the Lord Jesus. Then Peter and John placed their hands on them, and they received the Holy Spirit.*
>
> (Acts 8:14–17)

There is nothing obscure about this passage. It is clear. One can be a true believer, baptized with water for the forgiveness of sins, and still not have the Holy Spirit.

Let us look at another story in the book of Acts that confirms the need to receive both baptisms. This time, the sacraments are reversed, which is an exception to the rule. But the basic rule is still the same: you need both baptisms—one in water for the forgiveness of sins and one in the Spirit for power.

Salvation of the Gentiles

While Peter was still speaking these words, the Holy Spirit came on all who heard the message. The circumcised believers who had come with Peter were astonished that the gift of the Holy Spirit had been poured out even on the Gentiles. For they heard them speaking in tongues and praising God. Then Peter said, "Can anyone keep these people from being baptized with water. They have received the Holy Spirit just as we have." So he ordered that they be baptized in the name of Jesus Christ. (Acts 10:44–48)

There is one clear difference in this story compared to the other two. The order of baptisms is reversed. Instead of first being baptized in water, the Gentiles were baptized in the Holy Spirit. But both baptisms occur. Peter did not feel that being baptized in the Holy Spirit was sufficient; he called for water baptism, too. It was quite clear that God had to first pour out His Spirit upon these Gentiles, because the apostle Peter was reluctant to accept them as they were. God had to prove to Peter that even Gentiles could be saved without adhering to Jewish tradition.

I read a book of a well-known pastor who wrote about the Holy Spirit. I knew his theology—he believed that upon conversion a person received the Holy Spirit. Curious, I read his explanation of this same Scripture passage. He wrote:

> The story of the Samaritans was an exception to the rule that believers automatically receive the Spirit at conversion. For some reason, we do not know why, they failed to receive the Spirit at their conversion. Today, believers always receive the Holy Spirit when they are saved. The story of the Samaritans is an exception to the rule.

His statement is not true. The numerous Scripture passages I've presented prove otherwise. This well-known pastor is a good man; however, his teaching on water baptism is simply wrong and dangerous. It is even demonic. Satan will try every strategy to keep believers from seeking the baptism in the Holy Spirit.

The Three Cases

These three conversions (see Acts 19:1–7, Acts 8:14–17, and Acts 10:44–48) remind us of the need for new converts to receive the Holy Spirit. Do not merely accept the forgiveness of sins; go further by receiving the Holy Spirit. As you can see, Satan has done a good job deceiving believers, getting them to believe that they do not need to receive the Spirit after they are saved. Reject that lie. He may be trying to keep you from receiving your weapons of warfare. But now you know the truth. You need the Spirit after salvation. Only when Jesus received the Spirit did He have power over Satan, and you need the same Spirit to defeat Satan in your life.

FIVE

BAPTISM IN THE CLOUD

> *They were all baptized into Moses in the cloud and in the sea.*
> —1 Corinthians 10:2

Pastor Robert Morris of Gateway Church in Dallas, Texas, said that this passage convinced him of the need to be baptized in the Holy Spirit. Like many evangelicals, he'd assumed that he had received the baptism in the Holy Spirit upon his salvation experience. But when he saw that the Israelites were baptized *"in the cloud"* and *"in the sea,"* he recognized the difference between the two baptisms. One is from heaven; the other is on earth. When the Holy Spirit came, the Bible says there was *"a sound like the blowing of a violent wind…from heaven"* (Acts 2:2). The Holy Spirit *"came from heaven"*; thus, baptism in the cloud portrays baptism in the Holy Spirit.

Greater Baptism

> *I baptize you with water for repentance. But after me will come one who is more powerful than I, whose sandals I am not fit to carry. He will baptize you with the Holy Spirit and with fire.* (Matthew 3:11)

John clearly differentiates between his earthly water baptism and the greater baptism in the Holy Spirit. Furthermore, John said that the One who would come would baptize with the Holy

Spirit and is *"more powerful than I."* So the baptism with the Spirit is more powerful than water baptism. They both have their graces: water signifies repentance, but the Spirit brings power and purging from sin. *"His winnowing fork is in his hand, and he will clear his threshing floor, gathering his wheat into the barn and burning up the chaff with unquenchable fire"* (Matthew 3:12). Baptism in the Holy Spirit can burn chaff—the dry, scaly protective casing of seeds of grain—that water cannot. This takes us back to the analogy of the new birth, in which we become sheaves of grain. But with the sheaves comes useless chaff that needs to be burned away from our lives. Baptism in the Holy Spirit can do this.

I was a Christian before my baptism in the Holy Spirit. Unfortunately, I was not a good example to my friends and peers at school. I partied with them, committed some minor vandalism, cussed, and did other embarrassing things. All the while, I attended church and people would have said that I was a Christian. I suppose I was, but it was not until I was baptized in the Holy Spirit that I made a huge turnaround. No longer was I that old, dirty kid doing everything everyone else seemed to be doing. The Holy Spirit burned away the chaff in my life. He made me compassionate toward those caught in sin. I do not recall doing so, but people tell me that during my early walk with Christ, I would weep when I talked with people about Jesus. I was the weeping teen evangelist. My heart broke when I saw the bondage of my peers, and it broke even more when they rejected Christ. There is no way that I could have developed such passion for Christ and compassion for others on my own. It took the Holy Spirit to bring this in my life.

The great evangelist John G. Lake wrote about his own baptism in the Spirit:

> Personally I knew that my sins had been blotted out, but it was only two months prior to my Baptism in the Holy

Ghost that I learned by the Word of God and experienced in my life the sanctifying power of God subduing the soul and cleansing the nature from sin. This inward life cleansing was to me the crowning work of God in my life at that period. I shall never cease to praise God that He revealed to me the depth by the Holy Ghost, the power of the blood of Jesus.[3]

This doesn't mean that a Spirit-filled Christian is without sin or incapable of regressing back to his old way of life. Yet the Holy Spirit guards the Spirit-filled Christian from completely turning from the truth and rejecting Christ. Giving us the baptism in the Holy Spirit was God's way of making us holy like Him, so that He could keep us near Him. Reverend Lake said, "The forces of our personality must be subdued unto God." He credits his renewed personality to the baptism in the Spirit. Hopefully, many reading this book will recognize their own need for a change.

With my permission, a well-known Christian psychologist from Malta conducted a personality test on me to see what kind of person I am, or could be. After asking me a series of strange questions, she finished. I asked her, "So do you have an idea of the kind of person I am?"

She said, "Pastor Tom, I am so thankful that you were saved and filled with the Spirit, because you have the personality of either a great moral leader or mafia boss."

I laughed. "I don't doubt it, but God has changed my personality and character. Only He could have done it."

Baptism in the Holy Spirit subdues our personality and makes us into holy people. We all have the choice of going to the dark side or to the light side. The Holy Spirit helps us choose the light.

---

3. Taken from John G. Lake's sermon "The Baptism of the Holy Ghost."

Do not belittle the burning fire of the Holy Spirit. We need this unquenchable fire to deeply change us. Baptism in the cloud can do this.

Perhaps you have been baptized with water. Just as clearly as you know you were baptized with water, you also should know, without a doubt, that you were baptized with the Holy Spirit.

SIX

THE SEAL

One of the greatest benefits of receiving the Spirit is having an assurance of salvation. Satan will work overtime to cause you to doubt your salvation, and many Christians have lost their minds doing so. The devil is the *"accuser of our brethren"* (Revelation 12:10 KJV). He works hard to keep the believer in limbo over his or her salvation. But when the Holy Spirit comes, He banishes the doubts of the believer.

> *In whom ye also trusted, after that ye heard the word of truth, the gospel of your salvation: in whom also after that ye believed, ye were sealed with that holy Spirit of promise.*
> (Ephesians 1:13 KJV)

> *He anointed us, set his seal of ownership on us, and put his Spirit in our hearts as a deposit, guaranteeing what is to come.* (2 Corinthians 1:21–22)

A *"seal"* is the proof or evidence of ownership, such as a title deed. In biblical times, it was common for slave buyers to mark or pierce their slaves to seal them as their own. Today, ranchers do something similar to their cattle, branding them as their own.

The purpose of the seal is to prove or confirm ownership purchase, not to conduct an ownership purchase. Paul uses the term *"confirmed"* in connection with the work of the Holy Spirit: *"Our testimony about Christ was confirmed in you. Therefore you do not lack any spiritual gift as you eagerly wait for our Lord Jesus Christ to be revealed"* (1 Corinthians 1:6–7). The confirmation was the spiritual gifts—*"spiritual"* because they come from the Spirit.

The word *"confirmed"* was also used in this passage: *"So Paul and Barnabas spent considerable time there, speaking boldly for the Lord, who confirmed the message of his grace by enabling them to do miraculous signs and wonders"* (Acts 14:3). The Lord *"confirmed"* their work with *"miraculous signs and wonders."* The signs did not make the message true, but they proved and confirmed that it was true. The gifts of the Spirit often provide signs of divine validation.

The Seal Comes After Salvation

As you can see, God will "seal" you, confirming that you belong to Him. It comes after our salvation. As Paul said, *"In whom ye also trusted, after that ye heard the word of truth, the gospel of your salvation: in whom also after that ye believed, ye were sealed with that holy Spirit of promise"* (Ephesians 1:13). Notice, when you were sealed *"after…ye believed."* This seal comes not *when* you believe in Christ but *after* you come to Christ. *"**After** that ye heard the word of truth." The New International Version* seems to imply that we receive the Spirit when we believe in the gospel, but the original Greek does not justify that. Here, Paul shows two experiences: first, trusting in the gospel *after* hearing the word of truth; and second, receiving the seal of the Holy Spirit *after* believing the gospel.

Jimmy accepted Christ at a youth retreat but he was still plagued with doubts of his salvation. After weeks of confusion, he heard the teaching of receiving the Holy Spirit and went forward in church to receive Him. Nothing dramatic happened; however, at the end of that week, his mother told him, "Jimmy, there is something different about you. You seem patient and friendly. You seem to care more about people. I can see you really have changed."

Prior to receiving the Spirit, his mother had always accused him of not really living the Christian life after salvation. It was only after he received the Spirit that she noticed a change in him. When his mom remarked on the change, Jimmy was permanently freed from his doubt. The Holy Spirit confirmed to him and others that he was really God's child. The confirmation of the Holy Spirit is a changed life.

Abba Father

> *You received the Spirit of sonship. And by him we cry, "Abba, Father." The Spirit himself testifies with our spirit that we are God's children.* (Romans 8:15–16)

This is the main work of the Spirit. He wants you to know, without a doubt, that you are God's child. This is what God did at Christ's baptism and infilling of the Spirit: *"At that moment heaven was opened, and [Jesus] saw the Spirit of God descending like a dove and lighting on him. And a voice from heaven said, 'This is my Son, whom I love; with him I am well pleased'"* (Matthew 3:16–17). Jesus was the Son of God before the Spirit of God descended on Him; but by receiving the Spirit, He received outward confirmation of His sonship, and so did others who heard His voice.

This is what the Spirit will do for you. You will know, without a doubt, that you are God's child. You won't be sure of your salvation merely because the Bible says so. You will have the solid testimony within your heart. Without the Spirit, you will not have this assurance. The gifts confirm that you are sealed.

My wife, Sonia, received the Holy Spirit at the age of fifteen when she was in Germany. After getting saved and being filled with the Spirit, she went to a pub with her high-school friends.

She looked around at people drinking and was struck with fear. She thought it was wrong for her to be in such a dark, gloomy place. She feared that she had lost her salvation. So she bowed her head and told the Lord she was sorry for being there, and then she opened her mouth and started praying in tongues, relieved when she heard it. *The Holy Spirit did not leave me*, she joyfully thought. Her speaking in tongues confirmed that she still belonged to God.

Cornelius and Household Are Saved

Peter preached the gospel to the house of Cornelius. He and his whole household, though all Gentiles, embraced the message. Up to this time, the apostles had thought that the gospel was only for the Jews. What convinced Peter that Cornelius and his family had been accepted by God and had received the Holy Spirit?

> *For they heard them speaking in tongues and praising God. Then Peter said, "Can anyone keep these people from being baptized with water? They have received the Holy Spirit just as we have."* (Acts 10:46–47)

How did Peter know that Cornelius and his household had received the Holy Spirit? "[He] *heard them speaking in tongues*" (Acts 10:46). The gifts of the Spirit are the *"manifestation of the Spirit"* (1 Corinthians 12:7).

Jesus received the Spirit, who manifested in the form of a dove. This manifestation was visible to both Jesus and others. When the Spirit comes, He manifests Himself to you by your senses, so that you and others may notice.

Catholic, Orthodox, and Anglican Christians cannot point to a church ceremony and say, "I am a child of God because I have been confirmed." No, you need more than that. You need the gifts of the Spirit to prove that you have the Spirit. Being anointed with oil is not proof that you are filled with the Spirit; only the real oil of the Holy Spirit proves that you are Spirit-filled.

No one can tell me that I am not saved or God's child. I have the seal! The Holy Spirit came into my life at that Assemblies of God church, and I have gifts of the Spirit that confirm His coming.

> *Because you are sons, God sent the Spirit of his Son into our hearts, the Spirit who calls out, "Abba, Father." So you are no longer a slave, but a son; and since you are a son, God has made you also an heir.* (Galatians 4:6–7)

Many Christians are living as slaves when they could be living as sons and daughters. Some are slaves to pornography, others to gluttony, still others to drugs and alcohol. But when you receive the Spirit, you are freed from bondage and given rights. The Spirit makes all the difference. You move up to a higher level as "heir of God and co-heir with Christ." (See Romans 8:17.) You begin to receive all that Jesus purchased for you at the cross. But you won't get there without receiving the baptism in the Holy Spirit.

Manifestation of the Spirit's Presence

> *And this is how we know that he lives in us: We know it by the Spirit he gave us.* (1 John 3:24)

> *We know that we live in him and he in us, because he has given us of his Spirit.* (1 John 4:13)

How do you know God lives in you? You don't simply point to the Bible or to another minister and say, "They told me that God lives in me." No! You have assurance because you received the Spirit, and with the Spirit comes sufficient evidence. The Spirit turns your faith into knowledge; you are a "knower," not just a "believer." You *"know that he lives in* [you]." You may "believe" God lives in you; *"faith is…the evidence of things not seen"* (Hebrews 11:1 KJV). But when the Holy Spirit comes in you, He brings the *"evidence."*

Make no mistake about the Holy Spirit: when He comes, He does not come silently. His grand entrance was *"a sound like the blowing of a violent wind"* (Acts 2:2). And He still makes noise of some sort. It may not be as dramatic as His first entrance, but when He enters a believer, He still manifests His presence. He wants everyone to know that person belongs to God.

The Seal of Approval

> *Do not work for food that spoils, but for food that endures to eternal life, which the Son of Man will give you. On him God the Father has placed his seal of approval.* (John 6:27)

The seal of approval is an official mark that reveals that something has been accepted. People look for a seal to confirm the quality of a product. For example, the Good Housekeeping Seal of Approval gives a recognized credential of acceptance. The same is true of Christ. We believe Him not simply because He declared that He was God's Son but because of the evidence that He was.

> *I did tell you, but you do not believe. The miracles I do in my Father's name speak for me.* (John 10:25)

You see, Jesus said the miracles of the Holy Spirit testified for Him. They were the outward signs of His Sonship.

Jesus said,

> *Why then do you accuse me of blasphemy because I said, "I am God's Son"? Do not believe me unless I do what my Father does. But if I do it, even though you do not believe me, believe the miracles, that you may know and understand that the Father is in me, and I in the Father.* (John 10:37–38)

Again, this emphasizes that the miracles Jesus did confirmed that His *"seal of approval"* (John 6:27) was from the Father.

Accreditation

> *Jesus of Nazareth was a man accredited by God to you by miracles, wonders and signs, which God did among you through him, as you yourselves know.* (Acts 2:22)

Another thing people desire is accreditation. Accreditation occurs when a person is recognized, authorized, and certified upon meeting a certain set of standards. For example, a school may already be quite good without accreditation, but accreditation gives it a recognized level of credibility. This is what the Holy Spirit does. He gives us accreditation, making our message acceptable to God, which also gives outsiders reason to accept the message of the gospel.

The best accreditation does not come from the Southern Association of Colleges and Schools but from the Holy Spirit. When the Holy Spirit works in you, your accreditation comes from heaven, which is better than any accreditation a school can give.

On a recent Sunday, a woman traveled from Washington, D.C., to my church in El Paso, Texas, to be delivered from the demons that tormented her. God showed up and performed a dramatic deliverance. Demons began to speak through her, saying, "I own her."

But I told them, "No, you don't. God owns her. Come out of her, now!"

She coughed up mucous for about ten minutes, but then she was freed. Later, she came up to the microphone and told her story of how she had been tormented by voices but was now free. She said, "I want you to know that Bishop Tom Brown is a real man of God. Listen to his teachings."

After the service, a young girl I had never met came up to me and said, "I feel afraid. I felt the demons in that woman attacking me. But I would not let them come inside. But could you pray that God protects me?"

I did, and she felt at peace.

This young girl was new to Christianity. She had never before experienced the power of God as she had that day. Many people were filled with godly fear after witnessing this event. The dramatic exorcism spoke volumes to those seeking to follow Christ. They saw for themselves the real power of God. That young girl recognized a real man of God through the exorcism.

Even though I have been ordained in the ministry, my accreditation comes from the Holy Spirit. It is sad that many ministers only have degrees from Bible schools; they do not have God's accreditation that is manifested through signs and wonders.

Jesus was criticized by the religious leaders for not having man's approval. Yet His accusers could not explain His miracles. The power of the Holy Spirit was His accreditation. And this is what the Holy Spirit will do for you, too. You will be accredited by the Spirit of power.

SEVEN

IS TONGUES THE EVIDENCE?

Perhaps the most controversial topic associated with baptism in the Holy Spirit is speaking in tongues. Some Christians believe that you must be filled with the Spirit to speak in tongues; others say no, you can have the baptism in the Spirit without the evidence of speaking in tongues. Let us open our hearts to the Word of God:

> And these signs will accompany those who believe: In my name they will drive out demons; they will speak in new tongues; they will pick up snakes with their hands; and when they drink deadly poison, it will not hurt them at all; they will place their hands on sick people, and they will get well.
>
> (Mark 16:17–18)

Speaking in tongues will always stand out as a unique gift of the Spirit. This gift does not appear in the Old Testament or even during Christ's earthly life. It is distinctive of the age of grace. Luke had good reason to record the gift of speaking in tongues as the premier gift that is given to new believers when they receive the Spirit. You see, other gifts, such as healing and miracles, were apparent in the Old Testament, but not speaking in tongues. If the disciples performed only miracles that had been performed in the Old Testament, how would that prove that a distinguished New Covenant had been instituted? Speaking in tongues was the sign that introduced the New Covenant, and it still demonstrates it today. Look how the gift of tongues characterizes the salvation experiences of new believers:

> *When the day of Pentecost came, they were all together in one place. Suddenly a sound like the blowing of a violent wind came from heaven and filled the whole house where they were sitting. They saw what seemed to be tongues of fire that separated and came to rest on each of them. All of them were filled with the Holy Spirit and began to* **speak in other tongues** *as the Spirit enabled them.* (Acts 2:1–4)

> *While Peter was still speaking these words, the Holy Spirit came on all who heard the message. The circumcised believers who had come with Peter were astonished that the gift of the Holy Spirit had been poured out even on the Gentiles. For they heard them* **speaking in tongues** *and praising God.* (Acts 10:44–46)

> *When Paul placed his hands on them, the Holy Spirit came on them, and they* **spoke in tongues** *and prophesied.* (Acts 19:6)

These are the three instances in which speaking in tongues is mentioned in the book of Acts. There are two other incidents of people first receiving the Spirit, but there is no mention of tongues or any other spiritual manifestation; yet the two examples imply some type of physical manifestation. The first example occurs when the apostles prayed for the newly converted Samaritans, that they would receive the Holy Spirit:

> Then Peter and John placed their hands on them, and they received the Holy Spirit. When Simon saw that the Spirit was given at the laying on of the apostles' hands, he offered them money and said, "Give me also this ability so that everyone on whom I lay my hands may receive the Holy Spirit."
>
> (Acts 8:17–19)

Although speaking in tongues is not mentioned in the passage, Simon did see some sort of undefined manifestation of the Spirit: *"Simon saw that the Spirit was given"* (verse 18). What did he see? There is no agreed-upon explanation, so we are left in the dark.

The second example occurs when Paul, whose former name was Saul, received the Spirit when he became a new believer:

> Then Ananias went to the house and entered it. Placing his hands on Saul, he said, "Brother Saul, the Lord—Jesus, who appeared to you on the road as you were coming here—has sent me so that you may see again and be filled with the Holy Spirit." Immediately, something like scales fell from Saul's eyes, and he could see again. He got up and was baptized.
>
> (Acts 9:17–18)

The only spiritual manifestation mentioned here is Paul's restoration of eyesight. Yet restoring his eyesight was only one of two things Ananias had come to do; the other was to lead Paul in being *"filled with the Holy Spirit"* (verse 17). Now, we do know that Paul spoke in tongues, for He wrote, *"I thank God that I speak in tongues more than all of you"* (1 Corinthians 14:18). So did he speak in tongues when Ananias laid hands on him so he would *"see again and be filled with the Holy Spirit"*? We do not know for sure; the only thing we know for sure was that Paul was filled with the Spirit and that He did speak in tongues, at some point or another.

Of these two examples, we do know that in one case speaking in tongues did occur in the candidate, Saul, later named Paul. In the case of the people of Samaria, they may very well have spoken in tongues, however, the Bible does not mention it specifically.

Speaking Tongues Is Normal

I think the biblical evidence is clear: when someone first receives the Holy Spirit, speaking in tongues is a common accompanying manifestation. I use the word *common* instead of saying that it always happens. God is sovereign and works differently with all people. You cannot put Him in a box and assume that He must always work in a certain way. However, in the record we're given by Luke, speaking in tongues is a normal and common manifestation of the baptism in the Holy Spirit. (See Acts 2:1–4; Acts 10:44–46; Acts 19:1–7.) Therefore, I encourage people to expect this gift.

Speaking in tongues is not the only manifestation of the Spirit Luke mentions. In the first example, he mentions the *"sound like the blowing of a violent wind"* (Acts 2:2) and *"tongues of fire that separated and came to rest on each of them"* (verse 3).

The second example is of Cornelius. The people filled with the Spirit did two things: They spoke in tongues and praised God. (See Acts 10:46.) Praising God is another sign of the Spirit.

And the final example of the disciples in Ephesus showed that the gift of prophesy accompanies Spirit baptism, as well: *"They spoke in tongues and prophesied"* (Acts 19:6).

These three examples of new converts all showed other manifestations, as well. I think we could conclude that, in addition to tongues, we can and should expect other manifestations of the Spirit.

Pentecostals Without Tongues

It seems almost heretical to speak of a Pentecostal believer who does not have the gift of tongues, but it happens. Church history is filled with people who were gifted in other manifestations of the Spirit. What are we to conclude? That they never received the Holy Spirit? Surely not, for how would they manifest the gifts of the Spirit without the Spirit? Of course they were filled with the Spirit. They simply did not have the common manifestation of tongues. As long as you exhibit even one manifestation of the Spirit, you can be sure that you have been baptized in the Spirit. One manifestation is confirmation that you are God's child. It is sad that the baptism of the Spirit, which is meant to give assurance that you belong to God, is often debated to the extent that some believers who do not speak in tongues are worried that they are not saved. So long as you have even one gift of the Spirit, you have the Spirit.

Don't be bothered if you have not spoken in tongues. Do you have other gifts of the Spirit working in you? If so, then rejoice that you have the evidence of the baptism in the Spirit. Maybe it is not the common evidence but it is still supernatural evidence.

EIGHT

HOW TO RECEIVE THE HOLY SPIRIT

At this point, you may be saying, "I get it. I believe in the baptism in the Holy Spirit. I want it now. How do I receive the Holy Spirit?"

Here is how you receive the Spirit.

Thirst for It

First, you must thirst for it.

> *On the last and greatest day of the Feast, Jesus stood and said in a loud voice, "If anyone is thirsty, let him come to me and drink. Whoever believes in me, as the Scripture has said, streams of living water will flow from within him." By this he meant the Spirit, whom those who believed in him were later to receive.* (John 7:37–39)

If you are not thirsty, you won't take a drink of water. If you are not interested in the Holy Spirit, you will not receive Him. It should be noted that Jesus told the disciples to wait for the Holy Spirit: "Do not leave Jerusalem, but wait for the gift my Father promised, which you have heard me speak about" (Acts 1:4). When I am hungry, waiting makes me hungrier. The longer I wait for something, the more I want it. This is how we must feel about the Spirit. You must deeply want Him, as if you could not live without Him. You are thirsty. If you do not thirst after Him, it is unlikely you will drink of the *"streams of living water."*

Ask for It

Second, you must sincerely ask for the Spirit, For in Luke 11:13, Jesus said, *"Your Father in heaven [will] give the Holy Spirit to those who ask him!"* You must ask. This word *"ask"* doesn't mean to make a simple, quick petition, but carries with it the idea of asking for something you crave. It is a desperate longing. It suggests such desperation that one asks until he receives his request. *The Amplified Bible* gives a more literal rendering of this passage: *"Your heavenly Father [will] give the Holy Spirit to those who ask and continue to ask Him!"* (Luke 11:13 AMP). Do not give up asking simply because you have not received the gift. Keep asking.

Someone once said to me, "Oh, I tried receiving the baptism in the Spirit. I asked, others prayed for me, but nothing happened. It's not for me, I guess."

This person has failed to understand that to ask for the gift means you will keep asking until something happens. The persistent person will not take no for an answer. If you are thirsty enough, and bold enough to keep asking, you *will* receive the gift of the Spirit.

Receive It

You must receive the Holy Spirit. God gives, but you must receive. To receive, you must yield your tongue to the Holy Spirit and let Him use it to give you a heavenly language. Many make it hard for God to bless them with the gift of tongues. They make up their mind to shut their mouths, so that if their mouth magically opens and a different language comes out, they know it is from

God. They don't want to think they are "helping" God give them the gift of tongues.

Listen, you are not a puppet by which God makes you talk in tongues as a ventriloquist makes a puppet talk. It does not work that way. You must still do the talking; God will give the power. *"All of them were filled with the Holy Spirit and began to speak in other tongues as the Spirit enabled them"* (Acts 2:4). *"Enabled"* means to provide the means. The Holy Spirit gives you the capacity to speak in tongues, but you must speak. It is not the Spirit that talks; it is you that talks. The Spirit is the power; you are the conduit. Let the gift flow through you. It is up to you when and where the gift of speaking in tongues manifests.

Believe It

Ultimately, what you need the most is faith. *"He redeemed us in order that the blessing given to Abraham might come to the Gentiles through Christ Jesus, so that by faith we might receive the promise of the Spirit"* (Galatians 3:14). The greatest evidence of receiving the Spirit is *"faith."* What is faith? *"Now faith is the substance of things hoped for, the evidence of things not seen"* (Hebrews 11:1 KJV). We have been talking about the *"evidence"* of the Spirit's indwelling, yet faith believes even when it has not seen any evidence. You receive the promise of the Spirit *"by faith."*

If you stop believing, then there is no faith to give "substance to the things you hope for." One translation of this verse says, "[Faith] *is the confident assurance that what we hope for is going to happen"* (Hebrews 11:1 NLT). You must not lose faith when you pray for the Holy Spirit. Keep believing.

Have Someone Lay Hand on You

Even though it is possible to receive the Spirit without the laying on of hands, it is recommended to have hands laid upon you. I believe it is best to have a true minister of the gospel lay his or her hands on you to receive the Spirit. Remember that Philip the Evangelist was a powerful minister and was used greatly in miracles (see, for example, Acts 8:26–39), including casting out demons, but the apostles were the ones who laid hands on converts for them to be filled with the Spirit (see Acts 8:14–17).

The baptism in the Holy Spirit became so important that by the second century, concerned and cautious to preserve the integrity of the experience, only bishops, overseers of the churches and often leading pastors, laid hands on new converts to receive the baptism in the Holy Spirit. Even today within the Catholic, Orthodox, and Anglican churches, bishops lay hands on new believers to impart the Holy Spirit.

The Bible, however, does not require you to have a bishop lay hands on you. Here is scriptural proof: Ananias was an ordinary disciple, yet he laid hands on Paul to receive the Holy Spirit.

> *In Damascus there was a disciple named Ananias....Then Ananias went to the house and entered it. Placing his hands on Saul, he said, "Brother Saul, the Lord—Jesus, who appeared to you on the road as you were coming here—has sent me so that you may see again and be filled with the Holy Spirit."*
> (Acts 9:10, 17)

This is proof that ordinary disciples can lay hands on others to receive the Holy Spirit; however, it is customary when ministers do it.

It is a blessing to receive the baptism in the Holy Spirit by the laying on of hands. Then when you have, step out in faith and start acting on the gifts of the Spirit that you have received, including speaking in tongues.

Pray this prayer to receive the Holy Spirit:

Father God, I thank You for saving me from my sins. I am Your child. Your Word says that if I ask You for the Spirit, You will give Him to me. I do not fear the gifts of the Spirit, for I know that they are good for me, and I want all the gifts You want to give me. So, right now, I ask you to give me the Holy Spirit. I receive Him into my life. I am being baptized in the Holy Spirit. I ask this in Jesus' name, amen.

Now, yield your whole body to the Holy Spirit. Begin first with your tongue by praising God. Then, after praising Him in your own language, start praising Him in the new language the Spirit gives you called tongues. You will see that this gift will likely come into your life. It is not the only gift to come; expect other gifts to follow. Satan will tremble as you say this prayer and receive the gifts of the Holy Spirit, knowing that you are being empowered with the weapons of warfare.

Now, since you have prayed for the Holy Spirit, it is now time to learn about the nine gifts of the Spirit that accompany Spirit baptism and will begin to flow through you. For how can you receive the gifts of the Spirit if you are unaware of them? In the next section, I am going to explain the gifts of the Spirit: what they are, how they function (giving examples of their workings), and how you can receive them in your life.

PART 2

THE GIFTS OF THE HOLY SPIRIT

NINE

IGNORANCE AND REJECTION OF THE GIFTS

> *Now about spiritual gifts, brothers,*
> *I do not want you to be ignorant.*
> —1 Corinthians 12:1

There was a time in my life when I was completely ignorant of the gifts of the Spirit and, therefore, did not have them in my life. I was saved, I loved the Lord, and I read the Bible, but there were still no gifts in my life. Ignorance is not bliss. Ignorance keeps you from enjoying all God's gifts. Furthermore, ignoring the Spirit will also keep you from experiencing His gifts. Blatant disregard for His gifts will surely keep you from walking in the power of the Holy Spirit.

Ignorance of the Gifts

First, let's look at why some people are ignorant of the gifts.

Those Who Are Uninformed

You cannot believe in something you have not heard about. "How can they believe in the one of whom they have not heard?" (Romans 10:14). Just as people cannot believe in Jesus if they have not heard of Him, so, Christians cannot believe in the gifts of the Spirit if they have not heard of them.

The goal of this book is to teach you about the gifts, including what they are, how they operate, and our part in their ministry. If you have never experienced the gifts of the Spirit, keep reading; you will learn what they are so that you can pursue and expect them in your life.

Those Who Are Misinformed

Some companies prefer to hire people right out of college to avoid having to "unteach" bad habits they may have learned at previous jobs. It is harder to unlearn than it is to learn.

Worse than being *un*informed is being *mis*informed, for you are less likely to accept correction than you are to learn something for the first time. When you learn something first, it becomes part of your belief system.

Let me be honest with you: It is possible that if you know little about the gifts of the Spirit, you may have learned some wrong things. If so, I hope this book will challenge you. Some of what I say will contradict things that you once were taught.

Some people are misinformed about the *meaning* of the gifts. They are taught that spiritual gifts are natural talents rather than supernatural abilities. For example, the gift of healing is quite simple to understand. However, if you are prone to discount miracles, then you may understand this gift differently than what Paul intended. Some Christians have actually taught that the gift of healing is merely the skill of a doctor. I appreciate doctors but Paul did not have them in mind when he mentioned the gift of healing. He was thinking more along the lines of the supernatural gift of healing that Jesus exhibited in His life.

Some Christians misinterpret speaking in tongues, teaching that it is the ability to speak in foreign languages. While learning foreign languages is commendable, Paul did not have them in mind when he wrote about speaking in tongues. He was thinking of unknown tongues that *"no one understands"* (1 Corinthians 14:2).

It is important to understand how the Bible interprets spiritual gifts; and remember, the gifts of the Spirit are given only to those with the Spirit. Doctors or foreign language specialists are indeed gifted, but they do not have the spiritual gifts by virtue of their skills alone. These gifts are only given to born-again, Spirit-filled believers.

Ignoring the Gifts

Ignoring the gifts is a big problem in some charismatic and Pentecostal churches. If any church should be operating in the gifts of the Spirit, it should be these types of churches. They know the gifts and understand how they work, but some churches ignore them anyway. Ignoring the gifts does not mean a person disbelieves them; it just means that he or she is not paying them any attention or, at least, any special attention or consideration.

I have seen this occur in many places. I hear great sermons, inspiring messages, and even faith-filled prayers, but the gifts of the Spirit are ignored. The leader and congregation of these churches give no attention to the gifts. It is not a priority in their faith walk.

Some people ignore the gifts on purpose, because they do not want to be jeered and teased. People in Jesus' day jeered and criticized Him. They accused Him of casting out demons by the prince of demons. (See Matthew 12:22–32.) If you are sensitive to criticism, you will be nervous, perhaps even embarrassed, to use the gifts of the Spirit.

Pastor Jeff wrote to me, and said, "We need you to come to Florida because we are tired of being a seeker-sensitive church. We want to be a Spirit-sensitive church." He realized that they were catering to the world rather than honoring the Holy Spirit.

I was preaching in Canada when a man came up to me, and said, "You have what I am looking for. I used to attend a Pentecostal church but left it to go to a seeker-sensitive church. I love the gifts, but my Pentecostal church was not leading many people to Christ, and the seeker-sensitive church was. I now realize, through your ministry, we can have them both."

I believe it is possible to be sensitive to both the culture and philosophies around me as well as to the Holy Spirit, first and foremost. This is what Paul had in mind when we wrote,

> *So if the whole church comes together and everyone speaks in tongues, and some who do not understand or some unbelievers come in, will they not say that you are out of your mind? But if an unbeliever or someone who does not understand comes in while everybody is prophesying, he will be convinced by all that he is a sinner and will be judged by all, and the secrets of his heart will be laid bare. So he will fall down and worship God, exclaiming, "God is really among you!"*
>
> (1 Corinthians 14:23–25)

Paul was sensitive to the church's abuse and ignorance of the gifts. He did not want the church to scare away unbelievers or uninformed people, so he warned them not to abuse the gift of tongues by using it without interpretation. Notice that Paul did not conclude that it would be best not to have any gifts; rather he stated that prophecy, when used properly, could convict people: "He will fall down and worship God, exclaiming, 'God is really among you!'" The gifts can touch non-believers.

When non-believers hear that God is healing people in my church, they are quick to attend the meetings. Divine healing is a great tool to reach non-believers.

To date, I have had four television producers approach me about the possibility of hosting my own reality TV show. Were they interested in me simply because I give inspiring sermons? No. It is because the gifts of the Spirit operate in my life. Television producers know that the public is interested in miraculous powers and deliverance from evil spirits. People seek evidence of a demonstration of the Spirit's power.

Finally, some people ignore the gifts, not out of embarrassment or fear, but out of blind neglect. They may not mean to ignore the gifts, but they get into a rut, becoming complacent, lazy, and apathetic. We all are prone to fall into a rut or routine. If we are not careful, we can become bored in our walk with God, and even in our church services. When a person is in a rut, his walk is predictable. Be open to the move of the Holy Spirit. Be open to healing and deliverance. Be open to the gift of prophecy. Let the Spirit do what He wants to do.

One of my elders, Rey, told me that a young man came forward to pray for his uncle, who was dying. Rey began to pray, "God shows me that your uncle is not going to die. No matter what happens, believe that God will do a miracle."

The man took Elder Rey at his word. It looked bleak. His uncle got worse, and his whole family said their good-byes. But this young man said to them all, "I have prayed for our uncle, and an elder at my church had a word from God that he would live."

The family believed and laid their relative in God's hands, asking for a miracle. Sure enough, the uncle made a speedy recovery and was healed. The healed man came to our church to celebrate his life, and he looked great.

Apostle Guillermo Maldonado is being used right now to stir the church to move in the supernatural. He is helping churches to get out of their ruts. Like him, I encourage my members to be attentive to the Holy Spirit, not to ignore Him but to let Him work in and through them. The devil is not afraid of stagnant

Christians; he is afraid of Christians moving in the gifts of the Spirit. Only when you pay attention to the Spirit will you see God work in your life and the devil leave your life.

TEN

THE BELLS
ARE HEARD AGAIN

At the turn of the twentieth century, there were few pockets of miracles and healings taking place in churches; by and large, most churches were stagnant and in a rut. They rarely saw any gifts of the Spirit. It wasn't until a few "holiness" preachers in Azusa, California, started to seek the baptism in the Holy Spirit that the modern Pentecostal movement began. Today, more than five hundred million Christians claim to be Pentecostal, making it the fastest growing segment of Christianity in the world. And the Pentecostal movement is even impacting large denominational churches. This modern-day move of the Holy Spirit is prophetic, and why it signals the impending return of Christ. Let me explain why.

I believe the answer lies in understanding the role of Jesus as our High Priest. High priests wore robes that had pomegranates and bells of pure gold wrapped around their hems, which symbolized the fruit and gifts of the Holy Spirit: the pomegranates symbolized the fruit of the Spirit; the bells represented the gifts of the Spirit. Thus, high priests symbolically wore both the fruit and the gifts of the Spirit. (See Exodus 39:22–26.)

Paul called the clanging cymbals on the robes the gifts of the Spirit: *"If I speak in the tongues of men and of angels, but have not love, I am only a resounding gong or a clanging cymbal"* (1 Corinthians 13:1). The clanging cymbals can be the gifts of the Spirit. The pomegranates are, of course, the fruit of the Spirit.

In the Old Testament, when the high priest would leave the people and enter into the holy of holies, the Israelites heard the clanging bells of his robe and, therefore, knew he was alive. The same is true of Christ. Jesus is our High Priest; He wore the garments of the fruit and gifts of the Spirit. After He died and was resurrected, He ascended into heaven to carry on the work of the High Priest. How did the disciples know that He was acting as God's High Priest when He entered heaven, carrying on the work *"in the sanctuary, the true tabernacle set up by the Lord, not by man"* (Hebrews 8:2)? It's simple: They could hear the bells at the hem of His garment; or, in other words, the active gifts of the Spirit confirmed that Jesus was alive and was interceding on our behalf as our High Priest. The disciples knew Christ was alive at God's right hand, because He manifested the gift of tongues and other various gifts. The gifts of the Spirit were proof that Jesus, our High Priest, was serving at the sanctuary in heaven.

Hold Your Breath

How, then, does this relate to the apparent disappearance of the gifts? And why do I say that the restoring of the gifts of the Spirit is a signal that Jesus is about to return again? Let me explain.

To understand this better, let us go back to the foreshadowing of Christ's priestly ministry. An Old Testament high priest would sacrifice a lamb and carry its blood into the temple, which contained two rooms: one called the Holy Place and the other called the Most Holy Place, or holy of holies. He would go behind closed doors and minister before the Lord in the first room. The only way the people outside the temple knew that everything was all right inside was by the ringing of the bells. As long they heard the bells, they knew the priest was alive and still ministering.

Then the high priest would enter the second room called the Most Holy Place—a little room behind a very thick curtain. When he went into that room, the thick curtain absorbed the sound of the bells so that they could no longer be heard. There was no confirmation that he was alive and everyone waited with bated breath. Was the priest still alive and ministering on their behalf before the Lord or was he struck dead?

After the high priest finished his work in the Most Holy Place, he would exit the room and return to the first room, the Holy Place. When this happened, the people could hear the bells again—confirmation that he was alive. Then the high priest would momentarily leave the temple to be seen by the people.

The Confirmation That Jesus Is Alive

How did the disciples know for sure that Christ was indeed still alive at God's right hand? They knew because they experienced the gifts of the Spirit. The clarion of the bells of Christ let all the people know that He was still alive and ministering before God on our behalf.

However, just as the earthly priest went behind the curtain into the Most Holy Place, so also Christ entered the Most Holy Place, where the bells could no longer be heard until He was ready to come out from the temple. So, for nearly eight hundred years (from the tenth century to the eighteenth century), Christ's bells—the gifts of the Spirit—were rarely heard. By faith, Christians believed that Christ was indeed alive and ministering as High Priest on their behalf, even though, except for an occasional and rare miracle, they had no supernatural confirmation to prove it.

But something happened in this past century. In 1906, a small group of hungry believers in Azusa, California, experienced the baptism in the Holy Spirit, with the evidence of speaking in tongues. People around the world flocked to that little mission to receive the baptism of the Spirit, which hundreds of thousands experienced. Since then, millions of believers worldwide have received the baptism in the Spirit, with the manifestations—or gifts—of the Spirit. This movement became known as "Pentecostalism," although it is also sometimes termed "charismatic"—the fastest growing religious movement in the world.

A little more than a century ago, you would not have been able to find many people speaking in tongues. Today, you can find them everywhere. More and more believers than ever before are being baptized now in the Holy Spirit. What is happening?

Jesus Came Out of the Most Holy Place

Could it be that our High Priest, Jesus, has exited the Most Holy Place, so that the bells can be heard again? And in just a short time, He will exit the temple and be seen by all. I believe this new, fresh outpouring of the Spirit is one of the final signs of Jesus Christ's return.

The disciples asked the Lord what was going to be the sign of His return. Jesus said many things will occur before the final sign: earthquakes, wars, famines, and even apostasy. But these are only the beginning of birth pains. They will happen first, but the end will follow them.

The final sign is this: *"And this gospel of the kingdom will be preached in the whole world as a testimony to all nations, and then the end will come"* (Matthew 24:14). The last sign is a worldwide revival. Notice He said that this gospel would be preached as a *"testimony"* or "witness." A testimony is undeniable evidence. Jesus said, "You will be my witnesses when the Holy Spirit comes upon you." (See Acts 1:8.) Essentially, He was saying that we will have supernatural proof that He is alive when the Holy Spirit comes upon us. The gifts of the Spirit will be our supernatural proof.

The church had supernatural proof for the first thousand years, but for eight hundred years afterward, the supernatural proof nearly disappeared…until now. We have supernatural proof because we can hear the bells. And we shall preach the gospel to the whole world as His witnesses. Then the end shall come and the Lord Jesus shall be revealed from heaven.

As much as Satan tries, he cannot obstruct our hearing. We truly are experiencing great signs and wonders from the Holy Spirit. Are you ready to participate in the last and greatest revival the world has ever seen? We are going to need this revival, because the Bible predicts a great falling away of believers just before Jesus returns. And the only weapons that will keep us from falling away are the gifts of the Spirit. You need to be ready to move in the supernatural gifts of the Spirit.

ELEVEN

GIFTS ARE SUPERNATURAL

When I was a young believer, I memorized the nine gifts of the Spirit by categorizing them into three groups.

- First are the gifts of revelation: the message of wisdom, the message of knowledge, and the distinguishing between the spirits.
- Second are the gifts of power: faith, miracles, and healing.
- Third are the gifts of speech: prophecy, tongues, and the interpretation of tongues.

Although the categories may overlap a bit, I found that categorizing the gifts is a very helpful way to remember them. I hope it helps you, as well.

Trinity

> There are different kinds of gifts, but the same Spirit. There are different kinds of service, but the same Lord. There are different kinds of working, but the same God works all of them in all men. Now to each one the manifestation of the Spirit is given for the common good.   (1 Corinthians 12:4–7)

Paul begins his discourse on the gifts of the Spirit by highlighting the facts that, even before the coming of the Holy Spirit on Pentecost, God the Father and His Son, Jesus, have been imparting special gifts to us, His children. We receive these gifts at different stages in our lives. The three greatest stages are (1) when we are born, (2) when we were born again, and (3) when we were filled with the Spirit.

God the Father produced *"different kinds of working"* when each of us was born. Furthermore, Jesus the Lord imparted *"different kinds of service"* to each of us when we were born again. Last, the Holy Spirit gives us supernatural gifts when we are filled with Him.

1. God the Father gives natural talents at birth.
2. Jesus our Lord gives ministry gifts at conversion.
3. The Holy Spirit gives supernatural gifts at the baptism in the Spirit.

Before Pentecost, we were already endowed with certain abilities. I call the first endowment *natural talents*, since we were born with them. This includes personality gifts. Some are strong leaders, others are great organizers, and others are incredible singers. These abilities are given to us at birth. God the Father, our Creator, is responsible for imparting these abilities.

Then, when we are born again, Christ imparts certain *ministry gifts* to us. He may use natural talents, such as public speaking, to make someone a preacher, or He may transform a strong leader into a bishop. In other words, Jesus takes our natural, God-given talents we received at birth and uses them for ministry.

This book focuses on the third impartation of gifts in our lives, gifts we receive when we are filled with the Holy Spirit. Unlike the first two endowments, which could be considered natural abilities, the Spirit's gifts are *supernatural gifts*. Again, God may use a person's natural talent of speaking to make him a preacher, but the Holy Spirit can make that preacher's message supernaturally powerful. God the Father provided natural talents, but the Holy Spirit adds His "super" to your "natural" abilities. Thus, they are "supernatural."

Although we will not be dealing with natural gifts or ministry gifts, I do want to mention that the common denominator between natural gifts and the gifts of the Spirit is that they all are *gifts*. You had nothing to do with your natural gifting. You are naturally predisposed to act and perform a certain way. You can refine your talents by practicing the things you are good at, but you cannot give yourself natural talents. For example, I love to sing, but no matter how much I sing, I will never become a *good* singer. My vocal chords, voice, and lack of musical ability prohibit this.

Gifts are freely given and cannot be earned, and we have an obligation to cooperate with the Giver of our gifts. For example, you may be a good singer, and, if that is the case, you can perfect that gift by working to improve your voice and control. The same is true of the gifts of the Spirit. With God's help, you can work to perfect the gifts of the Spirit in your life, and I will show you how to do that. Satan will try to discourage you from growing in your gifts. Don't let him. Just as a shooter gets better with his weapon through practice, so too, you can improve the use of your gifts. You need to improve, otherwise, your weapons of warfare may be useless to you. Now let's look closely at the gifts of the Holy Spirit.

Manifestations

> *Now to each one the manifestation of the Spirit is given for the common good. To one there is given through the Spirit the message of wisdom, to another the message of knowledge by means of the same Spirit, to another faith by the same Spirit, to another gifts of healing by that one Spirit, to another*

miraculous powers, to another prophecy, to another distinguishing between spirits, to another speaking in different kinds of tongues, and to still another the interpretation of tongues. All these are the work of one and the same Spirit, and he gives them to each one, just as he determines.

(1 Corinthians 12:7–11)

Here, the first thing Paul mentions about the gifts of the Spirit is that they are "manifestations" of the Spirit. To "manifest" is to make known what is unseen; to make something clear, evident, or apparent, usually to the sight but also to any of the physical senses. The Holy Spirit is invisible, yet He can manifest His power and wisdom through His gifts. Just as the Spirit was manifested in the form of a dove at Jesus' baptism, so He also manifests Himself in other ways, through the gifts of the Spirit.

Definitions

The apostle Paul does not define the nine gifts of the Spirit. He simply lists them. Some are easy to understand, such as the gift of healing, but other gifts, such as the gifts of wisdom and knowledge, are more difficult to comprehend. Was Paul referring to a message that you receive *from* the Spirit or a message that you deliver *to* people? In defining gifts like this, I am not going to be dogmatic; arguing one way or another is counterproductive. Since words can have multiple meanings, I will endeavor to share with you the various understandings of the gifts of the Spirit, often from the classical Pentecostal viewpoint, and sometimes from a more evangelical one.

I will also do my best to share with you examples of how the gifts of the Spirit have worked and are working in modern society, both from my own life and the lives of others. I want this teaching to be revolutionary in your life. I want you to desire these gifts. I want you move in the gifts of the Spirit. Get hungry for more of God. Desire these spiritual gifts in your life!

Now we embark on learning about each of the gifts. I will explain them in the order that Paul lists them. Keep in mind that these gifts are your weapons of spiritual warfare.

TWELVE

MESSAGE OF WISDOM

*To one there is given through the Spirit
the message of wisdom.*
—1 Corinthians 12:8

The first gift on Paul's list is the *"message of wisdom."* It was the common practice in Bible times to list the most important thing or person first. Not all gifts are equal in importance. Some are greater than others. *"But eagerly desire the greater gifts"* (1 Corinthians 12:31). This is the case with the gift of wisdom.

By putting this gift before all the others, Paul shows that receiving and sharing wisdom is the greatest of all spiritual gifts. It is the number one spiritual weapon against Satan, and naturally so, because Satan's greatest attribute is wisdom. The Bible says that God created Satan *"full of wisdom"* (Ezekiel 28:12).

He is not particularly known for his strength, but he is known for his intellect. There is no way we can defeat Satan with our own wisdom. Eve tried and lost. Satan has a way with deception and can confuse even the smartest man. People have said that Stephen Hawking is one of the smartest men in the world, yet Satan fooled him by convincing him that there is no god. The Bible says, *"The fool says in his heart, 'There is no God'"* (Psalm 14:1). Stephen Hawking has been fooled by Satan, and if he is not smart enough to avoid Satan's deception, neither are you. You must rely on the wisdom of the Holy Spirit to defeat Satan.

Wisdom Is the Best Gift

If you asked Pentecostals what the best gift of the Spirit is, they might say tongues, healing, or miracles, but Paul says wisdom is the greatest gift. Pentecostals often favor demonstrations of healing and deliverance, and while these are important gifts—especially to the sick and possessed—the greatest gift is wisdom. *"Wisdom is supreme; therefore get wisdom"* (Proverbs 4:7). *"Supreme"* means the highest. Therefore, there is no gift higher than the gift of wisdom.

Solomon understood this perfectly well. God came to him in a dream and told him that He would give him anything he wanted; so Solomon prayed, *"Give me wisdom and knowledge, that I may lead this people, for who is able to govern this great people of yours?"* (2 Chronicles 1:10). Solomon asked for the two gifts Paul lists first: *"To one there is given through the Spirit the message of **wisdom**, to another the message of knowledge…"* (1 Corinthians 12:8). They go hand in hand. As a result of Solomon's asking for and receiving of wisdom, God gave him that which accompanies wisdom.

> God said to Solomon, *"Since this is your heart's desire and you have not asked for wealth, riches or honor, nor for the death of your enemies, and since you have not asked for a long life but for wisdom and knowledge to govern my people over whom I have made you king, therefore wisdom and knowledge will be given you. And I will also give you wealth, riches and honor, such as no king who was before you ever had and none after you will have.* (2 Chronicles 1:11–12)

What we see here is that riches and honor accompany the gift of wisdom. God does not give you riches and honor because you are a good boy and do not ask for them. Instead, the desires that people have—riches, honor, and long life—can all be obtained through wisdom.

When I was nearly twenty years of age, I came home one day after work and heard the voice of God. He said to me, "You can obtain wealth through wisdom." I had never heard that phrase before, and I was a bit shocked when God spoke this to me. I immediately protested; I could not believe that this was true. Then God took me to the Scriptures to verify His word to me. First he reminded me of Solomon's request for wisdom and how God also gave him wealth.

I thought, *Is there a difference between giving Solomon wealth **plus** wisdom, versus giving him wealth **through** wisdom?*

The Lord, knowing my thoughts, said, "Let Solomon's story tell you whether I gave him wealth *plus* wisdom or wealth *through* his wisdom."

> *Blessed is the man who finds wisdom, the man who gains understanding, for she is more profitable than silver and yields better returns than gold. She is more precious than rubies; nothing you desire can compare with her. Long life is in her right hand; in her left hand are riches and honor.*
>
> (Proverbs 3:13–16)

There was my answer. Solomon wrote that wisdom carries gifts in her hands: Long life is in her right hand, and riches and honor are in her left hand. In other words, if I receive wisdom, then I receive what is in her hands. Wisdom bestows *"wealth on those who love* [God] *and* [makes] *their treasuries full"* (Proverbs 8:21).

The gift of the right hand is more important than the gifts of the left hand. What is more important: long life or money? I think all of us agree that we prefer long life, and wisdom can increase your years. On the other hand, wealth and honor are less significant. Nevertheless, wisdom will supply those two, as well. These three blessings are perhaps some of the most sought-after blessings. People want long life, which is a result of good health, and they want wealth and respect. Wisdom comes with both.

Can you see then how important wisdom is? It may not be flashy or flamboyantly displayed like some of the other gifts, but it is the most important. Please do not gloss over this chapter to read about the more "exciting" gifts; perhaps wisdom is what you need more than anything right now, especially if you are facing a big decision that will affect the rest of your life.

+ Should you get married to this person or not?
+ Should you enter the ministry or not?
+ Should you stay with your spouse or not?
+ What school should you or your children attend?
+ What church should you join?
+ Should you remain at your church?
+ Where should you invest your money?

The answers to these questions can determine your success or failure. Satan would love for you to make the wrong decision so he can ruin your life and the lives of your family members and friends. But with God's wisdom, you can make wise choices.

Not Easy to Get

"*Though it cost all you have, get understanding*" (Proverbs 4:7). Wisdom is the most costly of all God's gifts of the Spirit. It is the most valuable, and it will often cost you "*all you have*" to get it. This is why many don't pursue it. They want wisdom and money and health, but not for the cost of all they have. Getting wisdom is too costly to most people.

The Hebrew word for *wisdom* is *chokmah*, which literally means "to pound something in." Wisdom is not obtained through osmosis. Instead, in a sense, it must be pounded into you. This process can work only in a submissive disciple, wanting to learn everything he or she can. Such a person is willing to go through humiliation, pain, suffering, correction, and anything else it takes to become wise. Without this humble attitude, you will not receive wisdom.

Knowing the Future

Wisdom is the ability to know how one's decisions and actions will affect tomorrow, the ability to see past today. *"Know also that wisdom is sweet to your soul; if you find it, there is a future hope for you, and your hope will not be cut off"* (Proverbs 24:14). But since none of us are God, who knows the future, we must depend on His wisdom to show us how our words and deeds will affect it. Wisdom will affect every area of your life: your finances, your marriage, your children, your ministry, and even your health. Though wisdom is spiritual, it is very practical, as well. It has real-world effects.

A Minister and His Son

A minister was losing the battle for his family. While his ministry was doing quite well, his rebellious teenage son was not. The minister tried everything he could to bring him back to the right path—he corrected him, rebuked him, got others to pray for him and talk to him—but nothing worked. He took the matter to God in prayer and asked for wisdom. God spoke to him and said, "The problem is that your son doesn't know that you love him."

Immediately he objected. "That's not so. I love my son."

"I know you love your son, but he doesn't know you love him. He thinks you don't believe in him. He thinks you are angry and disappointed in him. So let him know that you love him."

The minister took his son out to do one of his favorite activities. And toward the end of their fun time together, the father said to the son, "God spoke to me and told me that you don't think I love you. I am sorry for being so harsh. I think I gave you the wrong impression. I love you, Son, no matter what you have done or been through. I will always believe in you."

His son broke down in tears. From that moment on, the son made a 180-degree turn. He is now in charge of his father's ministry and is preaching the full gospel.

The point is this: God had to reveal the truth about the minister's son, and He gave the father practical wisdom. It produced a fabulous result. The minister says that he is now best friends with his son, and vice versa. They have a great relationship now.

The minister could have prayed over his son and rallied others to do the same, but in the end, what he needed was a simple, God-given message of wisdom. Of course, this example is not meant to imply that parents should not pray for, correct, and train their children, because they should; however, God warns, *"Fathers, do not exasperate your children; instead, bring them up in the training and instruction of the Lord"* (Ephesians 6:4). We should train and instruct our children in the way of the Lord; but we are cautioned not to go overboard in correction and thus *"exasperate"* our children. This is what the Holy Spirit revealed to the minister. Likewise, the Spirit can open our eyes to what direction we should take in every area of our lives. Wisdom is a spiritual weapon that can lead us into freedom.

A Congregant Recognizes Wisdom

Miguel and his wife had attended my church for over a year when we met for lunch and he said to me, "You know, Pastor, we came to your church because we knew about your deliverance ministry and we needed help. After being here for a year, God has changed us, but it was not through your gift to cast out demons. It was the wisdom you gave us through your preaching. I know people think your greatest gift is deliverance, but I think your greatest gift is wisdom."

I was humbled by Miguel's compliment. Even though others know me as an exorcist, I prefer to be known for my gift of wisdom. We can teach all day on the power-gifts of healing, miracles, and faith; but, often, what is often most needed is wisdom.

Even Jesus was not known only for his power-gifts. The people in Jesus' hometown asked, *"Where did this man get this wisdom and these miraculous powers?"* (Matthew 13:54). They recognized more than his *"miraculous powers"*; they also noticed His *"wisdom."* As a minister, you should not simply be known as a healing and miracle evangelist but as a wise evangelist.

It's even possible that the *"message of wisdom"* (1 Corinthians 12:8) Paul referred to was the preaching of God's Word. When preached properly, the Word is a message of wisdom.

This content of this book you have in your hands is the wisdom that God has shown me. Many travel from all around the world to come to my church so I can lay hands on them, but perhaps reading this book may be more helpful to your receiving what you need in your life. Remember, wisdom is the best gift, and I am sharing the *"message of wisdom"* with you right now. Receive it.

Imparting Wisdom Through the Laying On of Hands

God can impart wisdom not just through teaching but through the laying on of hands. *"Now Joshua son of Nun was filled with the spirit of wisdom because Moses had laid his hands on him"* (Deuteronomy 34:9). Most are aware that health is transferred through the laying on of hands. But wisdom can also come through the laying on of hands.

A minister from Africa came to my church. When we talked privately, he said he had come long distances and spent thousands of dollars because he wanted me to lay hands on him. I asked him what he needed, and he said, "I need wisdom. Lay hands on me like Moses laid hands on Joshua so that I can receive the wisdom God has given you." Wow! What a different prayer. He knew how important wisdom was compared to other gifts.

Joshua received great wisdom from Moses' prayer and was able to bring the Israelites into the Promised Land. He did this not only through might but also through wisdom. Although Joshua was a great warrior, his success was not solely dependent on his sword and spear. Joshua's wisdom was the key to spiritual victory for the Israelites.

Likewise, wisdom is the key to spiritual victory over Satan. You may be thinking that you need deliverance or healing, but remember what brought Joshua victory—his wisdom. Please do not discount the weapon of wisdom in defeating Satan.

The Serpent's Cunning

> But I am afraid that just as Eve was deceived by the serpent's cunning, your minds may somehow be led astray from your sincere and pure devotion to Christ. (2 Corinthians 11:3–4)

One of the best words that describes Satan is *"cunning."* You might think Satan is strong and powerful, yet he lost the battle with the archangel Michael. He is not nearly as *strong* as he is *wise*. To defeat him, you need to recognize his cunning.

Strong musclemen have handed over their wallets to thieves holding a fake gun. Intelligent people have lost their life savings to con artists. Bright men have been duped on social media thinking they were having a romantic affair with a beautiful model, when in reality, they were chatting with an old man.

If we can be deceived by people not nearly as smart as us, then don't you think Satan, who is far wiser, can deceive us, too? This is why you must depend on the wisdom of God.

Christine had eight demons and had the hardest time getting freed from them. Despite repeated attempts at deliverance, she wasn't freed until God gave her a special word of wisdom. When God spoke to her of her past abuse and the need to forgive the abuser, she understood why she hadn't been delivered! The demons came in through the door of her hatred of the perpetrator. While worldly people told her that she had every right to hate the abuser, God told her to forgive him. When she did, she was freed from all eight demons. Now she is totally committed to Christ.

The point of this story is that Christine was freed only when she received the wisdom of God. Jesus said, *"You will know the truth, and the truth will set you free"* (John 8:32). Often freedom comes only when we receive God's wisdom about a situation, and then we are set free.

The Book of Wisdom

The book of Proverbs is entirely devoted to wisdom. What other book in the Bible has only one theme? The Psalms, which is devoted to praise. Besides these two books, no book in the Bible is devoted to one topic. It seems to me that we should take wisdom (and praise) very seriously.

When I was a new believer, God told me to read one chapter of Proverbs a day. Since it has thirty-one chapters, it was a good read for each day of the month. As I look back, I now understand why God had me read it. He wanted me to receive the most important gift of the Spirit—wisdom.

How about you? Have you taken the gift of wisdom seriously? Are you willing to pay the price to get it? The Holy Spirit will impart it to you if you want it with all your heart.

One day, a foolish man came to a wise man and told him that he wanted wisdom. So the wise man took him to the river and plunged him into the water for about a minute. The foolish man was doing all he could to break loose from the wise man's tight grip. But finally, when it seemed the man could fight no more, the wise man lifted him out of the water.

He gasped and looked bewildered. After taking several deep breaths, he said, "Why did you do this to me?"

The wise man replied, "When you want wisdom as much as you wanted air, then you will get it."

How badly do you want wisdom? Ask and you will receive. Humble yourself so that God can "pound" His wisdom into you. You need it for spiritual warfare.

THIRTEEN

MESSAGE OF KNOWLEDGE

*To another the message of knowledge by means
of the same Spirit.*
—1 Corinthians 12:8

The *"message of knowledge"* is related to the gift of wisdom. This underscores how important the revelation gifts are to the Holy Spirit. The primary work of the Holy Spirit in a believer is to impart revelation. One of Paul's prayers shows this importance:

> *I keep asking that the God of our Lord Jesus Christ, the glorious Father, may give you the Spirit of wisdom and revelation, so that you may know him better. I pray also that the eyes of your heart may be enlightened in order that you may know the hope to which he has called you, the riches of his glorious inheritance in the saints.* (Ephesians 1:17–18)

Wisdom and revelation, and a heart being enlightened to the hope of Christ, were Paul's main requests. The body of Christ needs knowledge more than power. The more knowledge and understanding a person gets, the more he will walk in his inheritance and calling, and the more he will defeat Satan in this world.

The Spirit Guides into Truth

> *But when he, the Spirit of truth, comes, he will guide you into all truth. He will not speak on his own; he will speak only what he hears, and he will tell you what is yet to come. He will bring glory to me by taking from what is mine and making it known to you. All that belongs to the Father is mine. That is why I said the Spirit will take from what is mine and make it known to you.* (John 16:13–15)

The Spirit will guide us to two truths: first, knowledge of the future. *"He will tell you what is yet to come"* (verse 13). This corresponds to the wisdom of God. To recap, wisdom is the ability to know how one's decisions and actions will affect the future.

The second area of the truth that the Holy Spirit guides us into is our inheritance. Jesus said, *"All that belongs to the Father is mine. That is why I said the Spirit will take from what is mine and make it known to you"* (verse 15). How can the Holy Spirit take from what belongs to Christ to make it known to you? It's simple—all that belongs to Christ is yours.

Most Christians see only the wisdom side of the Spirit, as it pertains to direction in their lives—whether they should marry a particular person or not, should they move or not, should they take certain a job or not. That is the *wisdom* side of the Holy Spirit; but there is also the *knowledge* side of the Holy Spirit. While the Holy Spirit will lead you in making these very practical decisions, His main job is to lead you into knowledge of your inheritance. He will *"take from what is [Christ's] and make it known to you."* When you receive teaching that helps you understand and know what God has provided for you, you are receiving a message of knowledge.

Many believers have allowed Satan to afflict them with sickness and poverty simply because they do not know their inheritance in Christ. Knowing your inheritance is key to walking in victory over Satan. Knowledge of your inheritance as a child of God is a weapon against Satan.

The first weapon Paul tells the believer to put on is the belt of truth. *"Stand firm then, with the belt of truth buckled around your waist"* (Ephesians 6:14). Normally you would not think of a belt as a significant weapon. The same is true of knowledge. But when you know who you are in Christ—what you have in Christ and what you can do in Christ—then you have the power to defeat Satan. The old saying "Knowledge is power" holds much truth. As you grow in the knowledge of your inheritance, there is little that Satan can do to you.

No Eye Has Seen

> *However, as it is written: "No eye has seen, no ear has heard, no mind has conceived what God has prepared for those who love him"—but God has revealed it to us by his Spirit.*
>
> (1 Corinthians 2:9–10)

Nearly everyone has heard this Scripture before. And what people often take from this is verse that we can never know all the good things God has prepared for us until we die. Wrong! Notice that Paul said, *"But...."* This word is a conjunction, so we must keep reading. While it is true that no mind can know what God has prepared for us, the Holy Spirit can reveal it to us. *"But God has revealed it to us by his Spirit."* We have blessings revealed to us by the Spirit not after our death but while we are living.

So while there is no way that we can know what God has prepared for us on our own, God has given us His Spirit to reveal it to us. That is the work of the Holy Spirit. He opens our eyes to know what the natural mind cannot know on its own. Paul emphasizes the believer's need of the Holy Spirit to know these blessed things:

> *For who among men knows the thoughts of a man except the man's spirit within him? In the same way no one knows the thoughts of God except the Spirit of God. We have not received the spirit of the world but the Spirit who is from God, that we may understand what God has freely given us....The man without the Spirit does not accept the things that come from the Spirit of God, for they are foolishness to him, and he cannot understand them, because they are spiritually discerned.* (1 Corinthians 2:11–12, 14)

So, unless you have received the Holy Spirit, there is no way for you to *"accept the things that come from the Spirit of God."* In fact, you will consider the blessings of *"what God has freely given us"* to be *"foolishness,"* for you *"cannot understand them, because they are spiritually discerned."*

It is amazing that the Bible speaks so much about divine health and prosperity yet many people still reject them. Why? Because they have not received the Holy Spirit; so another spirit—the devil—deceives them into accepting sickness and poverty as their lot in life. Only through the teaching of the Holy Spirit can our eyes be opened to what *"God has freely given us."* Spiritual knowledge is a weapon to defeat Satan, who lies to us about our sickness and poverty.

Pancho is a member of my church. He grew up Catholic and then accepted Christ at a denominational church. Though this church preached salvation, he never saw the power of God to heal or prosper a person. For Pancho, attending our church has been a great learning experience. He has learned about his authority in Christ and the power of his words, that he can have what he says if it is in God's Word, for the first time.

He decided to put the teaching of positive affirmation to work in his life. He had been trying to sell a house for eight months and, after learning about his inheritance to prosper and the power of declaring God's Word over a situation, he said out loud, "In the name of Jesus, this house will sell in thirty days." Sure enough, it sold in thirty days.

He smiled at me during our meeting over lunch and said, "People ask me all the time if the miracles we hear about at Bishop Brown's church are real; I tell them, 'I'm not here to convince you; but I have seen it in my own life.'"

Maybe you are like Pancho. You have never heard about your inheritance. If that's the case, it's time for you to start receiving the knowledge of your inheritance in Christ.

Pentecostal Understanding of the Word of Knowledge

When a believer, often a minister, is given some unknown truth about a situation, Pentecostals classify this as a word of knowledge. A word of knowledge is usually in the form of a thought, impression, vision, or even the audible voice of God about a situation. For example, God may reveal to a minister that someone who is sick with lung cancer is being healed. This is a word of knowledge.

Word of Knowledge Examples

While I cannot confirm that the apostle Paul had this definition in mind when he mentioned the word of knowledge, there is ample scriptural evidence that God gives this supernatural information to people.

New Testament Example

A good example of this gift is seen in John chapter 1:

> When Jesus saw Nathanael approaching, he said of him, "Here is a true Israelite, in whom there is nothing false." "How

> *do you know me?" Nathanael asked. Jesus answered, "I saw you while you were still under the fig tree before Philip called you." Then Nathanael declared, "Rabbi, you are the Son of God; you are the King of Israel." Jesus said, "You believe because I told you I saw you under the fig tree. You shall see greater things than that."* (John 1:47–50)

Jesus did not have natural knowledge about Nathanael. He had never met him before, and no one had told Jesus about him; yet Jesus knew Nathanael. Nathanael was so shocked at Jesus' supernatural knowledge that he declared him the King of Israel.

Old Testament Examples

Saul's Destiny

A word of knowledge can shed light on a person's destiny, as in Saul's case:

> *Now the day before Saul came, the* L<small>ORD</small> *had revealed this to Samuel: "About this time tomorrow I will send you a man from the land of Benjamin. Anoint him leader over my people Israel; he will deliver my people from the hand of the Philistines. I have looked upon my people, for their cry has reached me." When Samuel caught sight of Saul, the* L<small>ORD</small> *said to him, "This is the man I spoke to you about; he will govern my people."* (1 Samuel 9:15–17)

The prophet Samuel knew exactly who would be anointed as king because it was revealed to him by the Lord. Likewise, God still reveals the direction Christians should take in their lives. Seek the Lord, and He will give you supernatural direction. You will know whether or not to go into business with certain people and, as in this case, who should be anointed and consecrated in the ministry.

Gehazi's Deception

The prophet Elisha healed commander Naaman of leprosy. Although Naaman wanted to pay Elisha for healing him, Elisha refused the money and sent him on his way to his own country. When he heard that Elisha refused Naaman's gift, Elisha's servant Gehazi tricked Naaman into giving him the gift instead. Gehazi tried to hide his deception from Elisha, but God revealed his act of greed to Elisha.

> "Where have you been, Gehazi?" Elisha asked. "Your servant didn't go anywhere," Gehazi answered. But Elisha said to him, "Was not my spirit with you when the man got down from his chariot to meet you?" (2 Kings 5:25–26)

This is a great example of a word of knowledge. Elisha was not physically with Gehazi when he caught up to Naaman and asked for his gift, but through the Spirit, he was able to see the whole thing. God can and still does use this method today.

Modern-Day Examples

A Man Caught Stealing

Something very similar happened to me recently. During a Bible study, I was listening to a guest speaker when the Lord spoke to me and said, "So-and-so is stealing the offering right now." I turned to my wife and told her to give me the keys to my office, where the offering was kept at that time.

She asked, "Is everything all right?"

I quickly retorted, "Just give me the keys!"

She reached in her purse, took out the keys, and handed them to me. Then I hurried out of the sanctuary. As I opened the doors leading down the corridor to my office, I saw that my office door was open. As I walked down the long hallway, so-and-so darted out of my office and went into the restroom. When he eventually came out of the restroom, I caught him with nearly $2,000 of loose bills stuffed in his pants. Church cameras confirmed his theft, and we also found some cash envelopes hidden under a desk.

This was no doubt a supernatural experience. There is no possible way anyone could deny the Spirit's working through me in this instance. The Holy Spirit still gives believers supernatural words of knowledge today.

Who to Anoint as Pastor

Recently, God spoke clearly to me about who I should anoint as our new Spanish pastor. I told that man, Lorenzo, what God had said to me and how he would be paid should he accept the position. He turned to his fiancée, Nadine, and said, "Didn't I tell you exactly what the bishop would ask me?" Then he turned to me and said, "I had a dream of this meeting, and in the dream, you spoke certain words to me, and I told Nadine what you would say to me. And you said exactly what I saw in the dream." This is a word of knowledge. God gave supernatural words to both Lorenzo and me.

Word of Knowledge That Brings Healing

A common area in which people have seen the word of knowledge operate is in divine healing. Here is a biblical example:

> And a woman was there who had been subject to bleeding for twelve years. She had suffered a great deal under the care of many doctors and had spent all she had, yet instead of getting better she grew worse. When she heard about Jesus, she came up behind him in the crowd and touched his cloak, because she thought, "If I just touch his clothes, I will be healed." Immediately her bleeding stopped and she felt in her body that she was freed from her suffering. At once Jesus realized that power had gone out from him. He turned around in the crowd

> and asked, "Who touched my clothes?" "You see the people crowding against you," his disciples answered, "and yet you can ask, 'Who touched me?'" But Jesus kept looking around to see who had done it. Then the woman, knowing what had happened to her, came and fell at his feet and, trembling with fear, told him the whole truth. He said to her, "Daughter, your faith has healed you. Go in peace and be freed from your suffering."
> (Mark 5:25–34)

Jesus felt power come out of Him that healed the woman who suffered from hemorrhage. He had no natural knowledge that anyone had been healed, only a sensation of the Spirit.

A similar experience happened to me one day while I was preaching. I felt power coming from my right hand, so I turned toward the right section of the audience and asked who felt the healing power of Christ. A young girl lifted her hand. She was healed by the power of God and no longer needed her two crutches. Her testimony was featured on television. Often, healing and a word of knowledge will work together. So do not think it strange when God reveals who or what He is healing.

Word of Knowledge as Instruction

> Now, brothers, if I come to you and speak in tongues, what good will I be to you, unless I bring you some revelation or knowledge or prophecy or word of instruction?
> (1 Corinthians 14:6)

Word of knowledge can be separate from teaching or it can be part of instruction. Good Bible teaching that contains revelation and supernatural knowledge is a manifestation of the message of knowledge. After hearing me preach, people have said, "You were reading my mail"; "I felt that God was speaking to me through you"; "I was meant to be here for the word you gave."

This is the message of knowledge. It is supernatural. Yet sometimes we fail to give proper credit to the Spirit who gives us this gift. Unless something unusual or dramatic takes place, we often do not think the Holy Spirit's gifts are in operation. Yet they are, so long as the message is controlled by the Holy Spirit. After hearing a great message at church, don't say, "The sermon was great, but the Holy Spirit did not manifest Himself. We did not see any gifts." Simply because you did not see a healing and miracle, such as the blind seeing, the deaf hearing, or the demon-possessed set free, does not mean that the Holy Spirit was not at work. Do not minimize the importance of the message of knowledge. It can come in various forms, including through a sermon or a simple message from one person to another. At times, you may be totally unaware that God is using your words to speak intentionally and directly to a person He has chosen.

Before we move on from the first two gifts on Paul's list, let us afford them proper importance. Other than the gift of His Son, there is no better gift that God gives us than wisdom and knowledge. Paul puts them on the top of the list of the gifts of the Spirit.

FOURTEEN

SPECIAL FAITH

> *To another [wonder-working] faith by the same [Holy] Spirit.*
> —1 Corinthians 12:9 (AMP)

The special faith Paul mentions is not the faith that saves us. Every believer has the faith to save; otherwise, he or she would not be a believer. Paul, however, is talking about miracle-producing faith that enables a person to receive a miracle from God or to do an unusual feat.

Saint Paul clearly showed what kind of faith he was referencing, because he mentions it here: *"If I have a faith that can move mountains, but have not love, I am nothing"* (1 Corinthians 13:2). Here he is talking about mountain-moving faith. To move a mountain is impossible by man alone.

Biblical Examples of Miracle-Working Faith

Moses Parts the Red Sea

Moses had this faith when he stretched his staff over the Red Sea. (See Exodus 14.) He was confident that God would show His salvation to Israel.

Daughter Freed of Demon Possession

The Canaanite woman in Matthew 15 was confident that her daughter would recover from demon-possession. (See verses 21–28.) Despite the fact that the disciples tried to chase her away, she would not lose faith. Her persistence showed the gift of "[wonder-working] faith."

When the Sun Stood Still

One of the greatest biblical examples of miracle-working faith is when Joshua made the sun stand still. Israel was battling five nations, yet despite its being outnumbered, it was winning. The problem, though, was that the day was ending, and Joshua was concerned that the five kingdoms would reorganize overnight. So he lifted up a crazy prayer:

> On the day the Lord gave the Amorites over to Israel, Joshua said to the Lord in the presence of Israel: "O sun, stand still over Gibeon, O moon, over the Valley of Aijalon." So the sun stood still, and the moon stopped, till the nation avenged itself on its enemies, as it is written in the Book of Jashar. The sun stopped in the middle of the sky and delayed going down about a full day. There has never been a day like it before or since, a day when the Lord listened to a man. Surely the Lord was fighting for Israel! (Joshua 10:12–14)

What a miracle! Joshua actually believed that God would delay the going down of the sun. He had miracle-working faith!

Daniel's Trust in God

Daniel exercised this special faith before an anxious king. After spending a night in the lion's den, Daniel said to the king, "O king, live forever! My God sent his angel, and he shut the mouths of the lions. They have not hurt me, because I was found innocent in his sight.

Nor have I ever done any wrong before you, O king" (Daniel 6:21–22). The king affirmed that David was not only holy but had great faith. *"The king was overjoyed and gave orders to lift Daniel out of the den. And when Daniel was lifted from the den, no wound was found on him, because he had trusted in his God"* (verse 23). There you have it: Daniel *"trusted in his God."* He exercised wonder-working faith.

God will send angels to accompany the gift of faith. I have seen this happen many times in my ministry. People have had visions of angels and Jesus during the services. Many have told me that they see angels and Jesus walking along with me while I was preaching. A man named Steve said to me, "Every time you moved your hand, the angel behind you would move his hand. I am not sure if he was imitating you or he was causing you to imitate him." These visions, I believe, are a result of the gift of faith, not only my faith but theirs, too.

Elijah Calls Down Fire from Heaven

Elijah had great faith when he called down fire from heaven to prove to the Israelites and the prophets of Baal who the true God was. He instructed the false prophets of Baal to build an altar and to call down fire from their god. Elijah would do the same, calling upon Jehovah, and said that whichever god answered with fire was the real God. After the false prophets failed on numerous attempts, it was Elijah's turn to call upon his God. Elijah intentionally made it "hard" on His Lord. He told the people to pour water on the sacrifice, then he called upon God to send fire. The fire God sent not only consumed the sacrificed but dried up the water, as well. (See 1 Kings 18:16–46.)

Present-Day Examples of Miracle-Working Faith

T. L. Osborn's Ministry in Africa

I don't suggest putting God to this kind of test, yet it worked in this case. I heard the story of T. L. Osborn, a man who was called to lead Africa to Christ. After an unsuccessful first trip, he went back after receiving the Holy Spirit, ready to lead Africa to Christ through signs and wonders. As he was preaching, a Muslim interrupted him, asking, "Why do you think Jesus is the Son of God?"

Rev. Osborn said, "The Bible says so."

"True, but the Koran says that He is only a prophet."

Osborn countered, "Bring the blind forward." Several blind people came forward, and he told the Muslim, "I give you a chance to prove whether or not Jesus is the Son of God or Muhammad is the prophet of Allah. Pray for these people, that, through Muhammad, Allah would open their eyes."

The Muslim declined.

T. L. Osborn laid hands on the blind, and they received sight. From that time on, Osborn's ministry took off in Africa. He won millions of souls to Christ through his miracle ministry. It began with the exercise of special faith.

You Got the Job

Years ago, I called various people to come forward for prayer during a Sunday service. A man named Raymond came forward and said, "Pastor, I need a job. I put in a job application this week, but I haven't heard from the business yet. I do believe God will give me the job."

I prayed for Raymond, and an unusual confidence came upon me. Although it was Sunday and we were at church, I told Raymond, "I am so sure you will get this job, and they will offer it to you before the service ends." I remember hearing myself say this and thinking, *How could they offer him the job now while we are at church?* (This was before cell phones.) Little did I know that Raymond had given the business our church number as a reference. Before the service ended, the church phone had rung, and the business owner had asked to speak with Raymond. The person answering the phone had called Raymond out of the service, and the owner had told him he got the job. Raymond immediately interrupted the service to tell about the phone call and my word of faith that he would get the job before the end of the service. This is an example of the gift of faith.

The Faith of Pastor Steven Furtick

Steven Furtick had just begun pastoring a new church in Charlotte, North Carolina, which was nothing to write home about, when he attended a Bono concert at the Time Warner Cable Arena. When one of the opening bands, U2, was playing the introductory riff to the "City of Blinding Lights," out of nowhere, Steven turned to his friend Erick and said by faith, "One day, our church will fill this arena for a worship service."

That statement sounded outlandish. How would a fledging church be able to fill that arena? But, four and half years later, they held an Easter Worship Service in that same place, and it was packed. This is an example of the gift of faith.

Smith Wigglesworth's Step of Faith

One of the greatest pioneers of the Pentecostal movement was Smith Wigglesworth. He may have had a funny name, but he was a serious apostle of faith—a gift he was known for. His ministry witnessed several cases of people being raised from the dead. He would often say, "If you will take a step of ordinary faith, when you come to the end of that faith, very often this supernatural gift of special faith will take over."

The trouble today is we want to wait until we feel faith before we act on it. Even though God has given us faith to move mountains, we often think we do not have enough faith. This was the way the apostles first looked at faith. They felt that it took a great amount of faith to move mountains. Here is their story and Jesus' response:

> The apostles said to the LORD, "Increase our faith!" He replied, "If you have faith as small as a mustard seed, you can say to this mulberry tree, 'Be uprooted and planted in the sea,' and it will obey you." (Luke 17:5–6)

At first, the apostles wanted to feel like they had great faith, but Jesus simply said that they did not need much faith to move a mulberry tree; a little faith can work big wonders. So start where you are; your little faith will become the gift of "[wonder-working] faith."

"He Is Not Breathing"

My wife and I were shopping at the Grapevine Mills Mall near the Dallas/Fort Worth International Airport, when we saw a man suddenly drop to the floor, banging his head hard on the ground. His wife fell on him, crying. We ran quickly to the scene, while a few others crowded around the man. Someone yelled, "He is not breathing." I could see that his chest was not rising and blood coming out of his ears and nose. His wife wrapped him in her arms, sobbing uncontrollably. Someone yelled for someone to call an ambulance.

I said to the wife, "I am a minister. Can my wife and I pray for him?" The wife happily consented. She moved off her husband to let us pray for him. We laid hands on him and commanded his spirit to return back to his body. We spoke life into him. As we did, he took his first breath and slowly opened his eyes. The bleeding from his ears and nose stopped, and he looked at me and asked, "What happened?"

"You fell hard on the floor."

He looked surprised. "I feel fine." As the emergency crew arrived, they instructed the man to stay lying down, but he said to them, "Let me get up; I feel just fine." Eventually, it became clear that he was fine. The man's wife hugged and thanked us for our prayers.

I thought the man died when he fell; I saw no life in him. But I also knew that with God, all things are possible. I did not feel such overwhelming faith, but when my wife and I spoke life into him, our faith, though small like a mustard seed, produced great results. It's been my experience that when I exercise my faith through words and deeds, whether or not I feel confident, great miracles take place. I think this is what Smith Wigglesworth meant when he talked about taking an ordinary step of faith. Take a step of ordinary faith, and then extraordinary faith will take over.

Like the stories you just read, you can be used to perform miracles with this wonder-working faith. But you will never get "special" faith until you use the "ordinary" faith that you have. Step out in faith, and God will move the mountains in your life.

FIFTEEN

GIFTS OF HEALING

To another gifts of healing by that one Spirit.
—1 Corinthians 12:9

One of Satan's top strategies of disabling Christians from fulfilling their calling is through sickness and disease. The Bible describes Satan as the author of diseases. So God has provided the spiritual gift of healing for us to overcome Satan's work of sickness.

The gift of healing is the ability of a Christian to heal another person. It is given not to the sick but to a person to heal the sick. This gift works very much in my life. Here are three stories in which God has used me to heal others.

I was at a car wash the other day when the owner approached me and said, "You do not know me, but I attended a service in your church. I brought my son who had asthma to your church. After you prayed for him, immediately he was cured. This was over ten years ago. My son was picked as an all-star football player in El Paso and got a scholarship to play football. None of this could have happened without God using you to heal my son. I just want to thank you for your prayers."

In another story, my uncle laid at home sick. He was suffering for weeks from a profuse nosebleed. He could not get up to do anything without aggravating the condition, so he just lay there. When I heard about his illness, I went to his house.

"Uncle Charles," I said, "God can heal you right now if you believe. Will you let me pray for you?"

He was happy to let me pray for him, commenting, "What do I have to lose?"

The moment I prayed for him, the bleeding stopped. He started to feel around for the blood, but there was none. Afterward, for years, my uncle would tell my relatives how I had healed his nose. Of course, it was not me but God's power working through me.

The other story is of a woman named Alice who gave birth to a premature child she named Faith. Faith was born with severe lung problems. After several days, Alice was able to leave the hospital with her daughter, so long as she agreed to keep her infant on a breathing machine. One Sunday, Alice came to church holding her baby, who was attached to an oxygen tank. I laid hands on her baby. Alice had great confidence that her newborn infant had been healed, so she took Faith to the doctor on Monday and told the doctor that she believed that God had healed her daughter and that her baby no longer needed the breathing apparatus.

The doctor smiled and said, "Alice, I am not aware of any baby in her condition that could get off the breathing machine so quickly. She still needs it."

Alice replied, "No, doctor. I am sure God healed her."

The doctor tried to humor her. "Look, let me prove to you that Faith needs the machine. The moment I take her off the machine, you will see her turning blue. Watch what happens!" Then the doctor took Faith off the machine and waited for his prognosis to come true. But Faith continued breathing without the machine.

The doctor was puzzled. He waited longer, but still Faith breathed fine. "I haven't seen anything like this before. But please take the machine in case her breathing gets bad." Faith continued to breathe normally. After many years, Faith continues to attend our church, and I recently baptized her in water. She is now a wonderful teenager serving God.

Stay Humble

One of the greatest challenges you will have in the healing ministry is not becoming disappointed when people are not healed but staying humble when people are healed. Here is a good story to illustrate this problem:

> *In Lystra there sat a man crippled in his feet, who was lame from birth and had never walked. He listened to Paul as he was speaking. Paul looked directly at him, saw that he had faith to be healed and called out, "Stand up on your feet!" At that, the man jumped up and began to walk. When the crowd saw what Paul had done, they shouted in the Lycaonian language, "The gods have come down to us in human form!" Barnabas they called Zeus, and Paul they called Hermes because he was the chief speaker. The priest of Zeus, whose temple was just outside the city, brought bulls and wreaths to the city gates because he and the crowd wanted to offer sacrifices to them. But when the apostles Barnabas and Paul heard of this, they tore their clothes and rushed out into the crowd, shouting: "Men, why are you doing this? We too are only men, human like you."* (Acts 14:8–15)

Truly, I can see the danger of someone taking pride in the gift of healing. When you have this gift, people will make sacrifices to see you. At this point, it is easy to think you are special. But Paul and Barnabas kept the people from worshipping them; they acknowledged, as we must do, that they were just human vessels.

One of the things I like to do when people are healed through the laying on of hands is to ask them who healed them. They are quick to recognize and proclaim that it was God and Jesus who healed them. This puts everything in perspective, giving God the proper glory, and fosters gratitude in the healer and the healed.

Since health is a very treasured gift, people will spend their whole life savings in acquiring it or maintaining it. This poses a great problem to those who have the gift of healing. If you have this gift, people may offer you money so that you can heal them. You must always decline and do it for free. Jesus said, *"Heal the sick, raise the dead, cleanse those who have leprosy, drive out demons. Freely you have received, freely give"* (Matthew 10:8). The fact that Jesus talks about giving *"freely"* in connection with the healing ministry shows that He knows our temptation of taking money for healing the sick or, at the very least, taking credit for healing others.

Remember the story of Elisha and Naaman recounted in chapter 13 on the word of knowledge? Elisha was used by God to heal Naaman. After Naaman was healed, he offered money to Elisha, who turned it down. Unfortunately, Elisha's deacon, Gehazi, didn't like Elisha not taking the money, so he secretly pursued Naaman for the gift. As a result of his greed, Gehazi contracted the same illness that Naaman had been cured of. This is a clear warning about using the gift of healing for monetary gain.

Skeptics

The gift of healing has its skeptics. One day I was preaching in the convention center in my city when I felt the anointing of the Holy Spirit coming from my right hand. So I looked at it and said, "There is someone receiving the power of God to heal them." This sensation is exactly what Christ felt when a woman touched the hem of His garment and He felt *"power [that] had gone out from him"* (Mark 5:30). Power to heal the sick was coming out of me, and a young woman named Cynthia who had recently got into a car accident lifted her hand and said, "It's me!"

She had arrived at the convention center with two crutches under her arms. It was quite clear she was unable to walk. But as I walked toward her, the power started to increase. She began to weep and shake as I approached her. She stood up on her own, and I took her by the hand and instructed her to walk without the crutches. She walked several steps, and I could feel that she was not even using my hand to help her. I let her go, and she began to walk, lifting her hand and praising God for healing her.

I had given permission to a man to videotape the service with his home camera. Later the next week, I asked the man if I could have a copy of his tape so I could air it as a commercial on television. He granted me permission, and we aired the healing of Cynthia on television.

The first showing of the commercial elicited a call from a man claiming to be a lawyer. He said, "I just saw your commercial, and I wanted to let you know that a church has hired me to sue you for lying."

I laughed. "How could you sue me when the woman was actually healed?" I prodded him, saying, "The first thing you are going to have to do is meet the woman who was healed. This way, you can gather all the evidence you need to prove your case."

He reluctantly asked, "Are you saying you will let me meet the woman?"

"Of course, if she doesn't mind. I have nothing to hide. God really healed her."

The lawyer said, "Look, I do not believe that God can heal anymore, so I am skeptical when someone claims to have healed someone. Do you understand that if this miracle was real, everyone in El Paso should be going to your church?"

Needless to say, that man was afraid to meet the healed woman, to have his skepticism countered. Cynthia appeared with me on television to talk about her miracle.

The lawyer represents many people who are skeptical of God's healing power. There is nothing in the Bible that should cause them to doubt; on the contrary, Jesus commanded us,

> Go ye into all the world, and preach the gospel to every creature. He that believeth and is baptized shall be saved; but he that believeth not shall be damned. And these signs shall follow them that believe; in my name shall they cast out devils...they shall lay hands on the sick, and they shall recover.
>
> (Mark 16:15–18 KJV)

Jesus expected many of his disciples to *"lay hands on the sick, and they shall recover."* This is part of the Great Commission. It includes preaching the gospel and baptizing people as well as the laying on of hands and healing the sick. This is our job. We have an obligation to believe, receive, accept, and do.

Jesus Emphasized Healing

Jesus healed many who had various diseases. (Mark 1:34)

The healing ministry of Jesus is in striking contrast to the prophets of the Old Testament. While certainly some of the prophets healed, their healing ministry was unusual and the healings rare. Yet Jesus' ministry of healing was a normal and, quite possibly, a daily work in His ministry. Indeed, with Jesus, the supernatural is normal. And with the same Holy Spirit living inside of us, the supernatural should be normal to us and our church.

Those with the gift of healing should use it regularly. There is a great need in our day for the healing ministry. Please do not limit healing to the human body, however. The literal Greek for

"Gifts of Healing" is "Gifts of Healings." "Healings" is plural. This shows that people need healing not just in their bodies but in their minds, relationships, and emotions, as well. Some need healing from panic attacks and manic depression. Others need healing in their marriage. So our ministry of healing must affect every realm that suffers sickness and disease.

One of Satan's top weapons is sickness. The Bible describes him as making people sick. It is no wonder that the gift of healing is a powerful antidote to Satan's weapon of sickness. Satan is dreadfully frightened of the gift of healing. This is why he tries so hard to raise skepticism in people about this gift. Don't fall for his tactic of doubt. Believe God can use you to heal the sick and remove Satan's blight on people's lives.

Do you feel that God is moving you in this ministry? Yield to His call! Be faithful. Do not doubt. And above all, stay humble when God uses you in this gift.

SIXTEEN

WORKING OF MIRACLES

> *For to one is given by the Spirit…the working of miracles.*
> —1 Corinthians 12:8, 10 (KJV)

This gift is not the gift of "miracles" but the *"working of miracles."* This means that you take part in this "work" of miracles. As Moses stretched out his rod and God split the sea, so you will have to "stretch out your rod." There are at least two main players in the work of miracles: God and you. Too often, though, we want to step back and let God do it all, but this is not scriptural.

God empowers you to work the miracle. So God needs you, a vessel, for Him to work through. *"For we are labourers together with God"* (1 Corinthians 3:9 KJV). God labors, but He does not labor alone to do the miracles. He needs you on earth to manifest His miracles.

"In the church God has appointed first of all apostles, second prophets, third teachers, then workers of miracles" (1 Corinthians 12:28). Notice that God has appointed these people in the church—not just the early church but the present-day, universal church.

Old Testament Examples of Miracles

The prophets of the Old Testament were often used in the working of miracles. For example…

- Moses threw down his rod, and it swallowed the serpents of Pharaoh's magicians. (See Exodus 7:12.)
- Moses spoke to the rock, and water gushed from it. (See Exodus 17:6.)
- Moses healed Miriam of leprosy. (See Numbers 12.)
- The priests in Joshua's time stopped the river Jordon when their feet touched the water. (See Joshua 3:15–16.)
- Samson defeated an overwhelming number of soldiers. (See, for examples, Judges 14:19; 15:15; 6:30.)
- Elijah multiplied the oil and flour of a widow. (See 2 Kings 4:1–7.)
- Elisha divided the river when he smote it with Elijah's mantle. (See 2 Kings 2:14.)
- Elisha raised a woman's son from the dead. (See 2 Kings 4:32–35.)
- Elisha cured Naaman from a skin disease. (See 2 Kings 5:10–14.)
- Isaiah healed Hezekiah's boils. (See 2 Kings 20:7.)

There are many more examples of Old Testament miracles, but those I have given show that people have a part to play in bringing miracles. These examples also show that miracles come in many varieties: from healings to resurrections to supernatural strength to defeat the enemy to even material provision. There is a miracle for every need.

The most commonly recognized miracle will be in the realm of health. Paul, after listing the *"gifts of healing,"* mentions the *"working of miracles."* These gifts overlap in many situations. So the working of miracles frequently includes the gifts of healing; however, miracles occur in other situations, as well.

The Miracle of Exorcism

The two most prominent miracles that Jesus performed were bringing health and deliverance. So the working of miracles also includes the ministry of deliverance. Let me give you one scriptural proof of this.

> *And the people with one accord gave heed unto those things which Philip spake, hearing and seeing the **miracles** which he did. For unclean spirits, crying with loud voice, came out of many that were possessed with them: and many taken with palsies, and that were lame, were healed.* (Acts 8:6–7 KJV)

Notice carefully the language used here: the people not only saw the miracles but "heard" the miracles: *"hearing and seeing the miracles which he did."* How did they hear the miracles Philip performed? The writer, Luke, explains, *"For unclean spirits, crying with a loud voice, came out of many that were possessed with them."* They heard the loud screams of the people being delivered. Also notice that the exorcism was called a "miracle."

The Greek word for "miracle" is the common word for power. Basically, it is the working of God's power in a person who needs His miraculous help. Philip simply "worked" God's power into the lives of the demoniacs. This is the working of miracles.

Adelle is an active member of our church, but her mother rarely attends the services. Adelle was concerned for her mother, so she arranged a meeting with me and invited her mother along. At the meeting, Adelle explained that her mom needed spiritual help, and I asked her mother what was going on. She broke down and confessed that she had a big drinking problem. After explaining a few things to her, I proceeded to pray. Soon the woman was screaming at the top of her voice. She was agonizing over the demons trying to control her, fighting and slithering on the carpet, and foaming at the mouth. I had never seen Adelle's mom act like this before; it was clear that demons had infiltrated her life. After about twenty minutes of praying for her, Adelle's mom was completely freed. Before this, she had rarely attended church, but since her deliverance, she rarely misses a service!

How many people are like Adelle's mom? Yet too often, the church is afraid to exercise God's power to set the captive free. There are more people in bondage than most people realize, and only God's power can liberate them.

Financial Help

The Old Testament prophets were often used to bring financial or material help to God's people. God blessed the Israelites with material provision. He sent manna and quail to the Israelites to meet their daily needs. (See Exodus 16:13, 15.) He used Elijah to multiply oil and flour to meet the needs of the widow from Zarephath. (See 2 Kings 4:1–7.) Jesus loved the story of the widow from Cain so much that He used it in His inaugural sermon.

Not only was Jesus' first sermon about God meeting the financial needs of a widow, but His first miracle was turning water into wine, meeting the material needs of the new groom and bride. (See John 2:1–11.) Then twice, Jesus multiplied bread and fish to feed the multitude. (See, for example, Matthew 14:13–21.) On another occasion, He told Peter to catch a fish and look in its mouth for tax money. (See Matthew 17:27.) Notice how often Jesus' miracles involved meeting people's material needs. God still does the same today.

Jesus said that Satan is a *"thief"* (John 10:10). Thieves generally still money or things with monetary value. Satan will try his best to rob God's children of needed resources to meet their needs and to help others. Miracles are God's way of getting back what

Satan steals from you. This is why the working of miracles is a weapon used against Satan.

God uses me a lot to pray for people to get jobs. I have had hundreds of people come to me for prayer concerning jobs—getting jobs, improving work conditions, receiving favor in the workplace, and getting raises. A man named Brian came to me recently and said, "Bishop, I would really like to stay in the El Paso area, but I can't find an engineering job. I have applied everywhere, and nothing has opened up."

"Brother Brian," I said, "God is going to give you more than one job offer. Let us pray." I prayed and prophesied that more than one job would open up for him.

The next Sunday, he came to me with a smile from ear to ear. "Bishop," he said, "I know you are not going to be surprised, but I got two job offers, and they both pay a lot of money."

So the only thing left to do was to pray for wisdom, that he would accept the right job. He took one of the jobs and found out that the top engineer knew me and that he was the only person in the southwest certified in a certain area; because of this, Brian began working toward this special certification. The working of miracles came through prayer for Brian!

Other Miracles

Don't limit the working of miracles to healing, deliverance, and material provision. God has many ways of bringing miracles to and through you. He can give you supernatural favor with others. He can lead you to a spouse even later in life. He can give you a child. He can open new opportunities that will launch you into greater blessings.

Don't forget, God can use *you* to bring miracles into people's lives. This is the working of miracles. Let God use you to change another person's life.

It's Work

One final note: The Greek word used for *"working"* as in *"working of miracles"* can be translated to our word *energy*. It is the common word for labor. No other gift of the Spirit is considered work but the one associated with miracles. I can verify that it often takes a great deal of work to eventually bring a miracle in a person's life. It is not always easy or quick. Sometimes you must work at length to bring the miracle in a person life. This is especially true regarding deliverance.

The deliverance ministry is not for the impatient. It is not for the easily discouraged. You will have to persevere in faith and not get discouraged when the miracle does not happen quickly in a person's life. But stay with it. Understand that God Himself warned you that the gift is the "working" of miracles, not the "watching" or "waiting" of miracles. It is true that good things come to those who wait, but greater things come to those who work.

The major work you must do is constantly pray for people until the miracle happens. For God to use you in the working of miracles, you must be willing to spend a lot of time praying for people. The miracle will not always happen in five minutes. Sometimes you will need to pray long for people. That is what makes the working of miracles very difficult. Be ready to work.

SEVENTEEN

PROPHECY

To one there is given through the Spirit…prophecy.
—1 Corinthians 12:8–10

The gift of prophecy is the ability to foretell the future by the omniscience of the Holy Spirit for the purpose of strengthening, comforting, and encouraging God's people. Prophecy will prepare God's people for any challenges they will face in the future; it will give guidance to God's people to prepare for any future events.

The desire to look into the future is quite alluring. People will fork out thousands of dollars to fortune tellers, psychics, or those claiming to have the gift of prophecy, just to know what their future holds. However, they are counterfeits of the true gift of prophecy. *"Let the prophets speak two or three, and let the other judge"* (1 Corinthians 14:29 kjv). Prophecies must be judged, but according to what standard? The New International Version translates the word *"judge"* as *"weigh carefully."* In order to weigh something, you have to put it on a scale. In biblical times, scales had two sides (like Lady Justice): one on which the seller would put a customer's purchase and the other on which he would put a few weights to see how much the product weighed. Some sellers were dishonest and used false weights; this is why the Bible says, *"The Lord abhors dishonest scales, but accurate weights are his delight"* (Proverbs 11:1).

So to have accurate scales, you had to put the accurate weight on the other side.

Likewise, in order to judge the accuracy of prophecy, one must weigh it alongside something accurate. The accurate weight is the Word of God. If a prophecy contradicts God's written Word, then it is a false prophecy, regardless of whether the prediction comes true or not. God even warned Israel of being fooled by false prophets, whose prophecies came true:

> If a prophet, or one who foretells by dreams, appears among you and announces to you a miraculous sign or wonder, and if the sign or wonder of which he has spoken takes place, and he says, "Let us follow other gods" (gods you have not known) "and let us worship them," you must not listen to the words of that prophet or dreamer. The LORD your God is testing you to find out whether you love him with all your heart and with all your soul. (Deuteronomy 13:1–3)

The ultimate proof that a prophecy is from God is whether or not the prophecy strengthens your relationship with the true God. The Bible warns about the misuse of prophecy more than the misuse of any of the gifts of the Spirit. This is why Jesus repeatedly warned, "*Watch out for false prophets*" (Matthew 7:15). Though the devil can deceive through healing and miracles, more often he deceives through prophecy. Thus, a very important weapon against Satan is the true gift of prophecy.

The Testimony of Jesus

"*For the testimony of Jesus is the spirit of prophecy*" (Revelation 19:10). True prophecy is centered on Christ. Some look to prophecy to find out which horse will win the Kentucky Derby or what lottery number will win the jackpot. However, true prophecy is focused on our relationship with Christ, not on winning megabucks or anything else.

Prophecy is intended by God to help His people deal with future situations. For example, the Bible tells the story of a prophet who predicted a famine: *"Agabus…stood up and through the Spirit predicted that a severe famine would spread over the entire Roman world"* (Acts 11:28). Why warn the church of an impending famine? The next verses explain why: *"The disciples, each according to his ability, decided to provide help for the brothers living in Judea. This they did, sending their gift to the elders by Barnabas and Saul"* (verses 29–30).

The prophecy was given to prepare God's people to send help to the brothers living in Judea. So when the famine took place, the saints in Judea already had a food supply, so the famine did not hurt them as much as it would have if they had not been prepared. The same principle could be found when God revealed in a dream to Pharaoh that there would be seven years of abundance followed by seven years of famine. Because the future had been revealed to him, and Joseph had interpreted the dream, the people of Egypt, including Israel's sons, were spared starvation. (See Genesis 41.) This prophecy set up Egypt to be the most powerful nation at that time.

Reverend Kenneth E. Hagin was warned by God about the impending recession of the 1970s, so he cut back his ministry's expenses; and, when the recession hit, it did not suffer. So prophecy is very helpful in preparing God's people for the future. Satan often creates circumstances to rob you of God's best; but through prophecy, God can help you avoid Satan's schemes.

Calling into the Ministry

> *While they were worshiping the Lord and fasting, the Holy Spirit said, "Set apart for me Barnabas and Saul for the work to which I have called them."* (Acts 13:2)

The Holy Spirit selected the right ministers in Antioch. In spite of his initial protest, Ananias was obedient to God and delivered His message to Paul: "*This man is my chosen instrument to carry my name before the Gentiles and their kings and before the people of Israel. I will show him how much he must suffer for my name*" (Acts 9:15–16). This prophecy gave Paul direction, so when his Jewish brothers rejected his message, he knew to go to the Gentiles. As history confirms, he became the greatest apostle.

God had spoken to me to pastor a church in El Paso, but my new bride, Sonia, was not convinced. We went to a new church that had just opened, and the pastor said, "There is a man that God has called into the ministry. Come forward."

I thought it might be me, but, as a visitor to the church, I was reluctant to go forward. Several people came forward, but the pastor said, "These are not the ones God is speaking to. You know who you are, so come forward."

Finally my wife said, "Maybe God is talking to you."

So I stood up and took my wife by the hand and said, "Let's go forward."

When I did, the pastor said, "It's about time you came forward. God was speaking to you all the time, and I knew you were the one that God had called into the ministry."

This pastor had never met me before. He did not know who I was. He had no idea that my wife and I were discussing pastoring a church. After he had prayed for us, God confirmed to my wife that I was truly called to begin a church in El Paso; so we did, and it has been a great success in both God's sight and in man's.

This Is Your Wife

Before I met Sonia, I had a vision. I was lying down on my bed when the ceiling turned into a movie screen. There I saw a woman with dark hair, but her face was blurry, and I heard God say, "This is your wife." My first thought was that I preferred blondes. I know this sounds carnal, but I think God revealed this to me to show me that God "preferred" Sonia for me.

Soon after I had the vision, I went to a nursing home to share the Word to the elderly. It was a ministry our church had just begun, and I had volunteered to help teach. It was during the second service we held at the nursing home that I met Sonia for the first time. I prayed, "Lord, is this the woman who was in my vision?"

I did not hear any heavenly voice confirm whether or not she was the woman in the vision. Later, however, the associate pastor, Jorge, came up to me and asked, "Who is that young girl with Maria?"

"That is Sonia. She is Maria's daughter."

Jorge said, "I asked you this because, the moment I saw her, I heard God say, 'This is Tom's wife.'"

Ever since, she has been the greatest blessing to me both personally and in the ministry.

A Prophecy of Marriage

Decades ago, several members came forward for prayer. I looked at one single man named Charles and gave him a prophecy: "You will soon find your wife." In just a few weeks, he met Connie, and they got married. Now they are happily married and have been faithful members of my church to this day.

A Good Fight

Timothy, my son, I give you this instruction in keeping with the prophecies once made about you, so that by following them you may fight the good fight. (1 Timothy 1:18)

Prophecies can strengthen our faith. How? Prophecies tell us what God wants to do with our lives; and in times when we doubt God's work and do not see the prediction coming true, we fight the good fight by reminding ourselves of the prophecies. Evidently, in the passage above, Timothy was not seeing the fulfillment of the prophecies in his life, so Paul told him to use the prophecies to stand in faith and expect what God promised to come true.

Prophecies do not necessarily come to pass immediately, so we must use those words from God to banish discouragement. It may be that God speaks to a wife that her husband will be saved, but she has yet to see the change. So the prophecy can help her avoid getting discouraged and throwing in the towel on her marriage.

The prophecy might be something about your ministry reaching many people for Christ, and you can use the prophecy to fight the good fight of faith, especially during times of discouragement or no evident fruit.

This is probably what Paul meant when he wrote, *"But everyone who prophesies speaks to men for their strengthening, encouragement and comfort"* (1 Corinthians 14:3). Prophecies can often do these three things: strengthen your faith, encourage you when you do not see the promises of God being fulfilled, and comfort you when God tells you that something saddening will happen.

For example, God prophesied to David through Nathan that his baby was going to die; and, when his baby died, David found comfort in knowing that God had a purpose. He did not give up on God, since He knew all things. In fact, when David found out that his baby died, he *"got up from the ground. After he had washed, put on lotions and changed his clothes, he went into the house of the* LORD *and worshiped"* (2 Samuel 12:20). The prophecy gave him comfort and helped him move forward.

The Last Days

Here are two biblical prophecies about the last days. Let me show you how to properly understand these prophecies.

> *But mark this: There will be terrible times in the last days. People will be lovers of themselves, lovers of money, boastful, proud, abusive, disobedient to their parents, ungrateful, unholy, without love, unforgiving, slanderous, without self-control, brutal, not lovers of the good, treacherous, rash, conceited, lovers of pleasure rather than lovers of God—having a form of godliness but denying its power. Have nothing to do with them.* (2 Timothy 3:1–5)

> *You must understand that in the last days scoffers will come, scoffing and following their own evil desires. They will say, "Where is this 'coming' he promised?"* (2 Peter 3:3–4)

What do these prophecies about the last days mean to us? They let us know that we are on the right track even when the world is on the wrong track. Today, more than ever before, we see immoral living, poor lifestyle choices being touted as holy and good, and hear more false teaching about God than ever before. So what do we make of this? If we had not known the scriptural prophecies given to us about these terrible, immoral, and irreligious times, we might go along with the crowd and join in with the immorality and scoffers of true Christianity. But instead, we are reminded by these prophecies to have nothing to do with the world and to stay true to God, even when the world seems to be straying further from Him. God has a plan; so we must not fail the tests in these last days. Indeed, the prophecies of the Bible help guard us against Satan's end-time plan.

Not only has God warned us that the world will get worse, but He has warned us that the church will be the hope of the lost world.

> *In the last days the mountain of the* LORD's *temple will be established as chief among the mountains; it will be raised above the hills, and peoples will stream to it. Many nations will come and say, "Come, let us go up to the mountain of the* LORD, *to the house of the God of Jacob. He will teach us his ways, so that we may walk in his paths."* (Micah 4:1–2)

People appreciate light more in complete darkness. God was predicting through prophets that in the last days, when the world gets darker, people will want a light. This is when the church can shine the brightest. So while God has spoken about the world, He has also told us that many nations will come to the church and say, "*Come, let us go up to the mountain of the* LORD....*He will teach us his ways, so that we may walk in his paths.*"

Misunderstanding Prophecy

Sometimes, prophecies can be misunderstood or appear incomplete, but when we hear of God's full plan, we receive strength, encouragement, and comfort. Here is an example of a prophecy that at first seemed discomforting but then proved comforting. The prophecy I am referring to is the predication of Agabus that Paul would be imprisoned. Let's see how this prophecy gave Paul strength.

> *A prophet named Agabus came down from Judea. Coming over to us, he took Paul's belt, tied his own hands and feet with it and said, "The Holy Spirit says, 'In this way the Jews of Jerusalem will bind the owner of this belt and will hand him over to the Gentiles.'" When we heard this, we and the people there pleaded with Paul not to go up to Jerusalem. Then Paul answered, "Why are you weeping and breaking my heart? I am ready not only to be bound, but also to die in Jerusalem for the name of the Lord Jesus." When he would not be dissuaded,*

we gave up and said, "The Lord's will be done."

(Acts 21:10–14)

The apostle Paul had a fuller understanding of the prophetic message. He knew it was God's will that he go to Jerusalem, even if it meant imprisonment. Why? Because he had heard a prophecy that he would suffer much and that it would result in testifying to kings. This came true for Paul; his chains advanced the gospel. (See Philippians 1:12–14.) He also preached in the palace of Caesar. (See Acts 23:12–26:32.)

I bring this up so that you do not assume you understand every aspect of a prophecy. A prophecy gives you one piece of a puzzle. And as you continue to walk faithfully in the word of prophecy, then God will enlighten you to understand more fully what He is doing in your life.

Not Always Prediction

Not every prophecy is a prediction of the future. Sometimes God will speak to you supernaturally or use you to speak supernaturally to another person without any mention of the future. The word may be meant simply to encourage you.

Here is one such example in my life. Years ago, I was ready to give up my church and do something else. I was really discouraged. I told my wife that I was ready to leave my city, and she cried. She knew I had experienced some real setbacks in the ministry, so she prayed.

It was Sunday night, my wife had gone to bed, and I had stayed up to watch Pastor John Osteen. As he preached, I thought, *Now John Osteen is the kind of pastor my church needs. They do not need me anymore.*

No sooner did I think this that John Osteen did something uncharacteristic: He stopped his sermon, looked directly into the camera, and said, "I am speaking to a pastor right now who is discouraged. You think you are not the man for the job, but you are. You are God's man for your church. Don't leave."

I was stunned, but I knew God had spoken to me. This is a form of prophecy, though it did not disclose any future events. It was a divinely inspired utterance. I thank God for the prophecy from Pastor Osteen, because it was used to banish Satan from my thoughts. So do not think that prophecy is always about the future. Sometimes it is just a message to encourage, comfort, and strengthen you. And Satan hates it when you are encouraged, comforted, and strengthened.

No One Knows

The most important future event is the return of Christ, and Jesus said that *"no one knows about that day or hour, not even the angels in heaven, nor the Son, but only the Father"* (Mark 13:32). If Jesus does not know when He is coming back, then what makes any prophet think he knows?

There have always been arrogant individuals that think they have pinpointed the time of the rapture or the second coming of Christ. One book on this subject that gained a lot of popularity is entitled *88 Reasons Why the Rapture Will Be in 1988*. A couple of my church members got caught up in this book. I had to correct them and tell them to quit distributing the book. They listened but, in the back of their mind, still thought it was true. Of course, as the year came and went, they realized the error of its author, Edgar C. Whisenant.

No one can prophesy or predict when the end of the world will take place. It is known only by the Father. Someone might ask, "Why has the Father kept this information from Christ?" We aren't told the answer. But what we do know is this: *"We have the mind of Christ"* (1 Corinthians 2:16), so if Christ knew, we would know. This is a secret that the Father has kept only to Himself.

Paul even had the same problems of people predicting the coming judgment in his day. He wrote, *"Concerning the coming of our Lord Jesus Christ and our being gathered to him, we ask you, brothers, not to become easily unsettled or alarmed by some prophecy, report or letter supposed to have come from us, saying that the day of the Lord has already come. Don't let anyone deceive you in any way"* (2 Thessalonians 2:1–3). It seems that pride gets the best of some people, for they want to be the ones to discover the *"day of the Lord."* It is not discoverable. If you think you know the day, hour, or even the year, then you have been deceived. Do not let others deceive you with any prophecy or prediction about the date of the rapture, the second coming of Christ, the end of the world, or the final judgment. No one knows but God the Father.

Satan Does Not Know the Future

People often ask me if Satan knows the future, and the answer is no. He is not omniscient like God. If he knew the future, he would have never inspired people to crucify the Lord. So one of the great weapons God uses against Satan is prophecy. God lets us know a little about the future so that we can be one step ahead of Satan.

EIGHTEEN

DISCERNING OF SPIRITS

To one is given by the Spirit the...discerning of spirits.
—1 Corinthians 12:8–10 (kjv)

Warner Brothers invited me to Hollywood for a special viewing of their movie *The Conjuring*. It's the true-life story of paranormal investigators Ed and Lorraine Warren, who attempt to expel a family of demons that were haunting their home. Since Warner Brothers recognized my experience in this field, they thought that I would enjoy it and therefore invite them to my church to show the movie, free of charge, to all the members, hoping that by word of mouth, the movie would be marketed throughout the community.

My daughter, Faith, joined me on this new adventure, and off we went on an all-expense-paid trip to Hollywood. A nice young girl picked us up at the airport and drove us to the studio. The first order of business was to sign an agreement not to disclose the plot or express an opinion until the film was released. Afterward we were kindly escorted to projection Room 2 for the private viewing. There were all sorts of amenities including extra-wide, comfortable chairs, but they were not going to convince me to endorse the movie unless I believed it had merit.

The first scene grabbed my attention as a few teenagers were tormented by demons that they believed to have come from a doll.

After some terrifying moments, Ed Warren got rid of the demons in the same way that I would have. So far so good.

I raised my brow, however, when Ed's wife, Lorraine, was given the title of clairvoyant—a person who supposedly sees or perceives things that are unseen. Frequently, clairvoyants claim to see or communicate with the dead. They are usually deceived and deceive others, projecting the work of familiar spirits.

Dead people are *not* roaming the earth, so there is nothing for clairvoyants to see. What they see could be familiar spirits that had once invaded a person's life, but they are demons, not human spirits. Deceased people have left this earthly realm and have gone to either heaven or hell.

Without giving too much of the plot away, Lorraine and her husband are called on to drive out a demon that is haunting the house of the Perron family. After investigating the work of this demon, Lorraine has a vision of the death of a child. She believes that the evil spirit is a mother who had murdered her child, and she convinces Mrs. Perron that this *spirit* is now trying to possess Mrs. Perron to get her to kill her children, as well. The mother becomes possessed but is later freed.

It seems to me that Lorraine planted fear in the mind of the mother. By saying that the spirit was trying to possess Mrs. Perron, Lorraine indirectly caused the demon possession. She planted a bad seed in Mrs. Perron's mind that bore terrible fruit and opened the door for the demon to come possess her. The demon could very well have been the spirit of murder, but this is not the same as a spirit of a deceased mother who roams the house to kill.

Needless to say, I was not able to endorse the movie because I felt that it would do more damage than good. Many people are highly suggestible or susceptible. The movie could cause many people to feel demon possessed, and some might seek help from the wrong people, such as clairvoyants, to rid themselves of demons.

I was told by the promoter that some priests endorsed the movie. I thought, *What kind of theology are these priests believing? Anyone who knows the Bible would recognize that it forbids the work of clairvoyants.* Scripture says, *"Do not turn to mediums or seek out spiritists, for you will be defiled by them. I am the* Lord *your God"* (Leviticus 19:31). Mediums are people who supposedly stand between the living and the dead, communicating the messages of the dead. God forbids any such activity or any activity of *"spiritists."* This covers any forbidden activity in the realm of the spirit. The reason God wants us to avoid these people is because God desires us to seek only Him when it comes to the realm of the spirit. And that is what the gift of the discerning of spirits is about. It is the Holy Spirit causing you to see, know, or perceive spirits. Only God should open your eyes to the realm of the spirit.

Burglar Alarm

The discerning of spirits is the ability to recognize the work of demons. Today, demons have been unleashed in alarming ways. They primarily work to deceive. I like what missionary evangelist Reinhard Bonnke termed the discerning of spirits. He called it "God's burglar alarm." When an intruder, or a bad spirit, tries to enter your life, the Holy Spirit will sound an alarm. He does this to protect you from the work of demons.

Teresa entered into a relationship with a man she met on Facebook who claimed to be from France. Since she had some knowledge of French, she was interested in him, but she told me that something inside of her just did not feel right. She was beginning to feel that this man was not who he'd claimed to be.

I told her, "I believe God is warning you about this man. I believe he is not from France, but from Africa." When I said that, she was shocked. She said that she had talked with him one time over the phone, and that his accent had not seemed French but African. After my warning, she immediately broke off the relationship, deleted him as a friend on Facebook, and blocked him. God had given Teresa discernment—sounding the burglar alarm inside her spirit, even before she spoke to me. God will do the same for you.

As you can see, when it comes to spiritual warfare, there is no gift of the Spirit more important than the discerning of spirits—the ability to see, know, or perceive the spirit that is responsible for a teaching, manifestation, or deed. This gift is very much needed in today's gullible world.

Judging

The Greek word for "discerning" is *diskrises*, which is derived from the word *krino*, meaning "to judge." Literally it means to judge whether something comes from God or Satan. But today, people do not want to exercise judgment. They prefer to tolerate any teaching or behavior, even if it does not conform to the holy and truthful standards of God.

Today we hear a lot about tolerance. Tolerance is the new morality of a world that has lost discernment. Tolerance is not love. Do parents love their children by letting them do drugs or sleep around or join a dangerous cult? That is not love. *"Love does not delight in evil but rejoices with the truth"* (1 Corinthians 13:6).

Today's "tolerance" is an attempt to show love without regard to right and wrong, truth and error. This is a distortion of God's character of truth and justice. Tolerance taken the wrong way could hurt others instead of helping them. This is why Christians cannot be tolerant in this way or politically correct according to today's devolved standards. If we did, we would open ourselves to deception.

In the book of Revelation, we find Jesus mentioning tolerance. In one case, He commends a church; and in another place, He corrects a church. What church do you think was commended and what do you think was corrected?

To the church in Ephesus, He said, *"I know your deeds, your hard work and your perseverance. I know that you cannot **tolerate** wicked men, that you have tested those who claim to be apostles but are not, and have found them false"* (Revelation 2:2). To the church in Thyatira: *"I have this against you: You **tolerate** that woman Jezebel, who calls herself a prophetess. By her teaching she misleads my servants into sexual immorality and the eating of food sacrificed to idols"* (verse 20). Isn't it interesting that the church that refused to tolerate wicked men was commended by Christ, and the church that tolerated Jezebel was corrected?

Today, if people exercise discernment when saying what is right and wrong, they are branded as judgmental. We need spiritual judgment. The reason we must have discernment is because Satan, his angels, and demons work to bring evil in the world. If the world were full of only good spirits, then we would not need the discerning of spirits. But there are many bad spirits in the world today that will try to lead people astray.

Deceiving Spirits

> *The Spirit clearly says that in later times some will abandon the faith and follow deceiving spirits and things taught by demons.* (1 Timothy 4:1)

We are in the *"later times,"* and demons primarily work to deceive; that is why they are called *"deceiving spirits."* How do they do it?

> *Such teachings come through hypocritical liars, whose consciences have been seared as with a hot iron. They forbid*

> people to marry and order them to abstain from certain foods, which God created to be received with thanksgiving by those who believe and who know the truth.   (1 Timothy 4:2–3)

Satan uses human beings to spread his lies; but the Holy Spirit gives you discernment to recognize whether a person's teaching is true. If people were able to recognize Satan, they would not be offended by your declaring that something is false; however, Satan is deceitful and uses people to twist the truth. So people may be offended if you discern a false teacher or teaching. You must have a strong backbone to operate in the discerning of spirits.

Meat of the Word

> But strong meat belongeth to them that are of full age, even those who by reason of use have their senses exercised to discern both good and evil.   (Hebrews 5:14 KJV)

The person who is feeding on the meat of the Word of God and living by it is the one who is most discerning of good and evil.

So the more you grow in the Lord, the better your *"senses"* will be *"exercised to discern both good and evil."* Discerning of spirits is not just discerning *evil* spirits but also recognizing the Holy Spirit and good spirits, as well. Someone who is very negative and feels like nearly everyone is wrong is not a mature believer feeding on the meat of the Word. They are usually babes in Christ who lack discernment.

Some people are so critical and negative that they think they have the gift of the discerning of spirits. Listen, the discerning of spirits is not the discovery that everyone is human and makes mistakes. That's a given! It is easy to spot the mistakes in others; it is much harder to spot the good. However, the believer feeding on the meat rather than the milk of the Word can see good spirits at work, too.

Conscious of Demon

Demons are real, but do not become obsessed with them. Some people have fallen into the error of becoming too demon-conscious. If they hear any noise in their house, they think demons are present. If they have electricity problems, they believe demons are manifesting in their house. They are not exercising the discerning of spirits but are rather being tricked by the devil, becoming obsessed with the supernatural. This is quite dangerous, too, just as it is dangerous to ignore demons.

It is my desire that you become so saturated and permeated by the truth of the gospel that you are fully aware of all your rights, benefits, defenses, and identity in Christ.

Visions

Discerning of spirits can include seeing visions of good angels. It is not always seeing the bad. Sometimes, the discerning of spirits works through visions and physical sensations. God can open your eyes to see angels and demons.

A woman named Kandra wrote to me, "I see angels and demons all the time. Someone told me that this is a gift of God. What do you think?" I wrote to her back and told her that it is not healthy for her or any person to experience constant visions of angels and demons. Someone who constantly sees demons is probably being tricked by the devil and needs psychological help. I have not seen any good come from people who constantly see visions of angels or demons. These visions can and do come, but they are rare.

As you can see, God is concerned about protecting you from evil, yet He encourages you to experience the good. Open your heart to God, who wants to give you the gift of discerning of spirits.

NINETEEN

TONGUES AND INTERPRETATION

To one there is given through the Spirit…speaking in different kinds of tongues, and to still another the interpretation of tongues.
—1 Corinthians 12:8–10

Last on the list of the gifts of the Spirit is speaking in tongues and its complementary gift of interpretation. The order of the listing is significant and indicative of their degree of importance. So this puts speaking in tongues and its interpretation as the least of all the gifts. Remember, Paul mentioned that some gifts are more important than others: *"Eagerly desire the greater gifts"* (1 Corinthians 12:31).

A man named Frank emailed me, "I have asked God to fill me with the Holy Spirit, yet I have not spoken in tongues. God uses me in healing, so why can't I speak in tongues?" Frank had a wrong view of tongues. Until he was able to speak in tongues, he felt inferior. He questioned whether he really had the Holy Spirit. Many Christians feel the same way as Frank. But be encouraged: If you have any of the gifts mentioned in 1 Corinthians 12, then you have the Holy Spirit. Remember, there is no possible way for you to manifest the gifts of the Spirit without first having the Spirit.

Personal Benefits of Speaking in Tongues

The reason the gift of tongues is mentioned last is not because it does not have benefits but because its benefits are private and personal rather than public and corporate. *"He who speaks in a tongue edifies himself, but he who prophesies edifies the church....Since you are eager to have spiritual gifts, try to excel in gifts that build up the church"* (1 Corinthians 14:4, 12). Speaking in tongues does not build up the church, unless it has been interpreted. Unless this happens, the only one who benefits from tongues is the one who speaks in tongues. Paul said, *"He who speaks in a tongue edifies himself."*

Personal edification is important, and that is why tongues is a great gift. It benefits the speaker. But since its benefits are limited to the one using the gift, Paul considers tongues the least of the gifts. All the other gifts benefit others. For example, the gift of healing benefits the person who is sick, not the one who has the gift to heal the sick. The same can be said of every gift of the Spirit except tongues. This is not to discount the gift of tongues but to put it in proper perspective.

The New Gift

Tongues is a very special gift because it is a new gift that represents the new covenant. None of the prophets in the Old Testament spoke in tongues. Jesus did not speak in tongues. (Of course, He did not need to because He knew all mysteries.) So tongues is a new gift and did not exist prior to the birth of the church.

The reason that God gave a new gift after Christ's ascension was to show the new covenant. With a new covenant came new gifts! If all we had were the same gifts available to the Old Testament prophets, then what would make the new covenant special or better?

When the first one hundred twenty disciples spoke in tongues, onlookers were bewildered; they had never seen this before. And Peter used this special gift to announce the fulfillment of the prophecies spoken by the prophets. He proclaimed, *"Fellow Jews and all of you who live in Jerusalem, let me explain this to you; listen carefully to what I say. These men are not drunk, as you suppose. It's only nine in the morning! No, this is what was spoken by the prophet Joel: 'In the last days, God says, I will pour out my Spirit on all people'"* (Acts 2:14–17). If the first one hundred twenty disciples had manifested only the gifts already recorded in the Old Testament, then Peter could not have linked the outpouring of the Spirit to the fulfillment of the new covenant. God gave a new gift to prove that the new covenant had begun.

What's So Special About Tongues?

Why is speaking tongues the gift that announced the new covenant? The answer is simple. Speaking in tongues signified a change from the old covenant way of conversion. Under the old covenant, if someone wanted to convert to Judaism, they would have to learn Hebrew. But under the new covenant, no one has to learn Hebrew; instead, God supernaturally gives people a language greater than Hebrew, a heavenly one. That is what speaking in tongues is. It is the language of heaven.

You do not learn tongues as you do other languages. It comes directly from the Holy Spirit. Paul calls it the "language of angels." (See 1 Corinthians 13:1.) There are languages of men and then there is the language of angels. Angels are part of heaven, and so speaking in tongues is a sign to the world of our spiritual birth.

How can you tell where a person was born? Not by skin color or clothes but by speech. Just as a person's speech reveals his or her birth place, so speaking tongues reveals that we are born again from heaven.

The Secret Prayer Code

The purpose of all languages, including the language of heaven, is to aid in communication. One of the most important tools of warfare is secret communication. If someone is in war, they need to secretly communicate with their own troops without the enemy hearing what is said. That is what tongues does for us. It is God's secrete communication language to God and angels. *"For anyone who speaks in a tongue does not speak to men but to God. Indeed, no one understands him; he utters mysteries with his spirit"* (1 Corinthians 14:2). Speaking in tongues is not an earthly language that people understand. But God and His angels understand it. When a person speaks in tongues, it actually becomes a prayer to God, which Satan cannot decipher.

The Gift of Tongues Baffles a Killer

A gunman entered an Atlanta school and began shooting. Fortunately, for the students and teachers, Antoinette Tuff was there to talk the young man into surrendering. She said to Diane Sawyer of ABC news, "I started interceding. I started praying in the Spirit." I believe God took her prayers in tongues and confounded the enemy within that man, the enemy failing to communicate his death plans to the man. Thank God for the gift of praying in tongues. Speaking in tongues saves lives.

It is a mistake to pray only in your own language. Satan knows what you are praying in your own language, so he works to prevent the answer. But when you pray in tongues, he has no idea what you are asking God. You do not necessarily know what you are praying, but you can be sure it is God's perfect prayer.

> *For if I pray in a tongue, my spirit prays, but my mind is unfruitful.* (1 Corinthians 14:14)

Prayer is divine communication to God, and that is what praying in tongues is—it is a believer's spirit communicating to God. Earthly languages are learned and come from the mind, but tongues is unlearned and comes from the human, born-again spirit. Tongues may be the lesser gift in terms of public benefit, but it is the greatest in terms of prayer.

Everyone Should Speak in Tongues

Since it is the highest form of prayer, Paul exclaims, *"I would like every one of you to speak in tongues"* (1 Corinthians 14:5). Paul longs for all people to speak in tongues. I believe it certainly is God's will for you to pray in tongues, as well. I see no reason why the gift of tongues should be withheld by God from any of His people. It seems logical that God would want all His children to communicate to Him in this most beautiful prayer language. Besides, we all need this secrete prayer code for spiritual warfare.

Let me give you some proof that everyone in the early church spoke in tongues as a prayer language and that this should get you to seek the gift of tongues for yourself. It appears that the whole church in Corinth spoke in tongues: *"So if the **whole** church comes together and **everyone** speaks in tongues…"* (1 Corinthians 14:23). The terms *"whole church"* and *"everyone"* suggests that every believer in Corinth spoke in tongues. I think this supports the argument that all members of the church can speak in tongues, if they yield themselves to this gift.

Though Paul longed for everyone to speak in tongues, he did not want the private gift to be publicly misused. Paul permitted the public use of the gift of tongues only when there was someone able to simultaneously or consecutively interpret the tongues.

If anyone speaks in a tongue, two—or at the most three—should speak, one at a time, and someone must interpret. If there is no interpreter, the speaker should keep quiet in the

> church and speak to himself and God.
> (1 Corinthians 14:27–28)

The gift of tongues is abused when a person takes what is meant for private and personal devotion and tries to use it in a public way. Paul discouraged the public use of tongues, unless it was interpreted. Tongues with interpretation, either by the speaker himself or an interpreter, becomes a public blessing. Of course, the interpretation would also let Satan know what was said, which sort of defeats the powerful benefit of tongues as being a secret prayer code to God. So Paul encouraged prophecy to be the normal gift for public messages. *"He who prophesies is greater than one who speaks in tongues, unless he interprets, so that the church may be edified"* (1 Corinthians 14:5). So tongues with corresponding interpretation, according to Paul, is equal to prophecy.

The Benefits of Speaking in Tongues

In addition to its private and personal use, speaking in tongues has several other benefits in your life.

1. Speaking in Tongues Makes You More like Christ.

> *But everyone who prophesies speaks to men for their strengthening, encouragement and comfort. He who speaks in a tongue edifies himself.* (1 Corinthians 14:3–4)

Speaking in tongues *"edifies"* people. Think of the word *edifice*. An edifice is a building, a work of construction, and our life is like a building. *"For we are…God's building"* (1 Corinthians 3:9). In effect, Paul was saying that when you speak in tongues, you act as a contractor building up your spiritual life. But our lives are not completely built yet. We are still in the process of *"being built into a spiritual house"* (1 Peter 2:5). God is not through with you yet.

Tongues, therefore, helps God build your life so that you are more like Christ. Notice in the above passage the words *"strengthening, encouragement and comfort."* Speaking in tongues will give you spiritual strength to withstand temptation. During times of trial, speaking in tongues will give you spiritual encouragement. And when heartache comes, you will be comforted by speaking in tongues. You may not realize that these blessings are being bestowed on you when you speak in tongues, but the Word says they are.

2. Speaking in Tongues Builds Your Faith.

Jude uses the same language when he talks about praying in tongues. *"But ye, beloved, building up yourselves on your most holy faith, praying in the Holy Ghost"* (Jude 20 KJV). Our faith is often weak. Doubts began to crowd our faith. Confusion begins to push out our confidence. But praying in tongues causes our faith to be built up. I am confident that the more you pray in tongues, the more your faith will grow. You may not associate faith with speaking in tongues, but the Bible confirms this.

3. Speaking in Tongues Strengthens Your Prayer Life.

So what shall I do? I will pray with my spirit, but I will also pray with my mind. (1 Corinthians 14:15)

Sometimes, you are not sure what to pray for, but the Holy Spirit knows exactly what you and others need from God. So when you are unsure of what to pray, start praying in tongues.

A woman came to me and asked me to pray for her son who was facing criminal charges. How do I pray? Do I pray that the jury finds him innocent? What about the victims? Should I pray that he serves time in prison? Maybe he is innocent. Would that serve God's purpose for him to be in prison? So I decided to pray in the Spirit. I explained to the mother that I was not sure what God wanted in her son's life but that I would pray in the Spirit and that God would use my heavenly language to accomplish His perfect will. She agreed. Later, the district attorney dropped the charges and her son started coming to church.

I don't pretend to know everything that God wants to do. I pray the best I know how. In the situations in which God's will is easily known, I pray specifically for it. But at other times, when I do not know what God wants to do, I pray in the Spirit. Praying in the Spirit also eliminates selfishness in prayer. We all can get selfish in our prayer lives, but when we pray in the Spirit, we always pray the perfect will of God.

Sometimes you will feel an urge to pray, but nothing will come to your mind. Or maybe a person or a situation to pray for comes to your mind, but you are not sure why you feel this urge. This is when praying in tongues is very beneficial.

Before I was married, my wife, Sonia, lived in another state. But God gave her an urgency to pray for me. She did not know what I was doing at the moment, but she prayed in the Spirit. Later, she asked me if anything dangerous had happened to me, and I told her that I had a very bad accident on a snow tube. Although I had flipped, I had landed perfectly well and had left without any serious injury. Is it possible that without Sonia's prayers, I could have been killed or seriously injured? Maybe. One thing is for sure, God will put people on our hearts to pray for; but when we do not know what they need, we should pray in tongues.

4. Speaking in Tongues Redeems Your Attitude.

I will sing with my spirit, but I will also sing with my mind. If you are praising God with your spirit, how can one who finds himself among those who do not understand say "Amen" to your thanksgiving, since he does not know what you are saying? You may be giving thanks well enough, but the other man is not edified. (1 Corinthians 14:15–17)

People lack gratitude. It is easy to focus on the dark periods of your lives without acknowledging the good times. Praying in tongues is a way to "praise God with your spirit." Often, when you pray in the Spirit, you are not even asking God for anything; you are simply praising Him and giving Him thanks.

In fact, the first incident of speaking in tongues in the Bible was of praise: "*We hear them declaring the wonders of God in our own tongues!*" (Acts 2:11). The one hundred twenty attendants in the upper room were "*declaring the wonders of God*" through speaking in tongues. Speaking in tongues is not just a prayer language; it is a praise language. It is a great way to praise God.

Satan will try to get you to become negative and complain. Negativity is His specialty. But as you praise God with your spirit in tongues, your attitude will change—you will feel positive and uplifted.

5. Speaking in Tongues Brings Rest.

Although speaking in tongues did not occur in the Old Testament, there were prophesies that it would happen. The apostle Paul referenced Isaiah 28 when he said, "*Through men of strange tongues and through the lips of foreigners I will speak to this people, but even then they will not listen to me*" (1 Corinthians 14:21). Let us look at the original passage in Isaiah.

> *Very well then, with foreign lips and strange tongues God will speak to this people, to whom he said, "This is the resting place, let the weary rest"; and, "This is the place of repose"—but they would not listen.* (Isaiah 28:11–12)

Notice Isaiah said that speaking *"strange tongues"* is the way to the *"resting place."* Those who are weary can rest in the Lord by praying in tongues. When you feel spiritually exhausted and have trouble walking in the ways of God, start praying in tongues, and you will find the rest that your soul longs for. You will be given divine direction and know where to go.

Over more than thirty years of walking with the Lord, it has been my experience that the more I pray in tongues, the more I am led by the Lord. When I fail to pray in tongues, I am prone to make mistakes. Please use this gift of tongues and pray often in the Spirit.

The Interpretation of Tongues

One final note: As previously mentioned, the gift of interpretation is a companion to the gift of speaking tongues. It is generally used in a public setting to explain the message in tongues. It not a translation of tongues, because how can you translate word for word a heavenly language? You cannot understand something spiritual, like tongues, by the language and interpretation of man. It is like trying to fit a round peg into a square hole. So it should be understood that an interpretation is not a perfect translation of tongues. However, it offers the general meaning of what has been spoken.

This explains why sometimes a message in tongues may last for thirty seconds but the interpretation lasts for two minutes. Do not think that something went wrong; it is not possible for human words to convey exactly what a speaker says in tongues.

> *For this reason anyone who speaks in a tongue should pray that he may interpret what he says.* (1 Corinthians 14:13)

No one better understands what a person says in tongues than the person who speaks it. After all, the spiritual message is conveyed through his spirit; so he should expect to get the essential word that God is saying to the people. However, God may use someone else to interpret the message.

Be bold and ask God for the interpretation of what you speak in tongues.

TWENTY

HOW TO ACTIVATE THE GIFTS

I remind you to fan into flame the gift of God, which is in you through the laying on of my hands.
—2 Timothy 1:6

Years ago, I took my wife and three children on a camping vacation to Colorado Springs. I had not been camping since my youth, so I was a bit inexperienced. We decided to go fishing, and after catching a few fish, we headed to the campground to cook them over a campfire. I had the most difficult time keeping the fire lit. I tried putting more twigs on it, but it did not help. Nothing I did kept the fire burning.

One of the men in the campsite saw my difficulty and came over with a flattened cardboard box, which used to fan the flame. I felt stupid. Immediately I recalled this passage in Timothy where Paul encouraged him not to let the fire of the Spirit go out but to purposely fan the fire to make it bigger.

We should want more manifestations of the Holy Spirit. And these manifestations will not happen without us "fanning the flame." I have seen many charismatic and Pentecostal churches lose the fire. They have become too sensitive to secularism and the anti-supernatural bias of the world. Thus, many are frightened of moving in the gifts of Spirit. This is nothing new. This is why Paul explained to Timothy that he was going to have to get rid of fear: *"For God did not give us a spirit of timidity, but a spirit of power, of love and of self-discipline"* (2 Timothy 1:7).

Timidity is the fear of people. Satan will try to get you to fear people, but you must face and conquer this fear if you want to move effectively in the gifts. In the ministry of deliverance, I have had to bear a lot of criticism, both from unbelievers who do not believe in the reality of demons and from Christians who do not like my style of deliverance. The point is, you are going to have to accept the fact that you will be criticized. Jesus was criticized for casting out demons and was even accused of being in league with Satan. If Jesus was criticized, then certainly you will be, too.

Promise Me One Thing

Norvel Hayes, a business man turned minister, is used extraordinarily in the gifts of the Spirit. He is not an eloquent man, but God uses him to heal the sick and cast out demons. As his ministry grew in popularity, God spoke to him, "Norvel, you must promise me one thing."

"What is it, Lord?" he said.

"Promise me that when you become big and famous, you will not stop casting out demons."

"Why would I want to stop doing that, Lord?"

"Many of my ministers cast out demons in the beginning. But when they become famous in the public eye, they stop casting out demons to avoid public criticism. Promise me, Norvel, you won't be like them."

Norvel promised, and he has kept his promise to God.

It is sad to see some people bow to the desire of social acceptance more than spiritual gifts, who evade and actually shun the supernatural gifts of the Spirit. These people are ashamed of the gospel.

Power, Love, and Self-Discipline

Paul told Timothy that, in place of timidity, God had given him *"a spirit of power, of love and of self-discipline."* The first gift God has given us to overcome timidity is power. Power means ability. Paul was reminding Timothy that in his own power, he could not manifest the supernatural, but that God had given him supernatural power. So it is with you: if you have received the baptism in the Spirit, you have power.

The second gift we are given to overcome timidity is love. There are two ways to understand the gift of love in Timothy's case: first, God loved Timothy, even when others hated him; second, Timothy was to use the gifts of the Spirit out of love for others. So long as you know that you are moving in the gifts out of your love to help others, you can have a clear conscience. The problem comes when you want to be noticed for your gifts. That's pride instead of love.

Paul also mentioned a third gift to overcoming timidity: self-discipline. You will need self-discipline to move effectively in the gifts of the Spirit. Sometimes people think that it is totally up to God when and how the gifts operate. But the truth is, you have a lot to do with how much and when the gifts will move through you. Yes, God is sovereign, but He works through human vessels. If He didn't, then why did Paul tell Timothy to *"fan into flame the gift of God"* (2 Timothy 1:6)? It is clear that we have a part to play in when, how, and how often the gifts of the Spirit will be activated in our lives.

You have to discipline yourself to move in those gifts in the same way that you have to discipline yourself in any other thing you are gifted in. Athletes may be great and gifted in what they do, but they still have to discipline themselves to get better. You have to do the same with the gifts of the Spirit. You will get better in operating in the gifts as you discipline yourself.

Quenching the Spirit's Fire

> *Do not put out the Spirit's fire; do not treat prophecies with contempt.* (1 Thessalonians 5:19–20)

Unfortunately, we can *"put out the Spirit's fire"* and hinder Him from moving. What's worse is that it is usually intentional.

A good friend of mine, Chas, who pastors in Houston, Texas, told me about his first encounter with a demon. He had just gotten saved at a large denominational church. His pastor told him that they believe in the whole Bible, so Chas assumed that included the parts about casting out demons. Later, Chas accompanied a group of people from the church to a restaurant when a woman in their party fell to the ground in the parking lot and appeared to be having a seizure. Chas was just a new Christian, but he had read in his Bible and knew that Jesus gave us authority to cast out demons, so he told the demons to come out. Eventually, the demons came out and the woman was freed.

The next day, Chas received a call from one of the pastors who asked to meet with him. The pastor told him that he heard about the encounter with the demon-possessed woman.

"Yes," Chas said. "Praise God that she was freed from the demons."

Then Chas received a rude awakening when the pastor said, "Brother Chas, I am glad everything worked out this time. However, we do not want you to cast out demons anymore from church members. We do not believe in this."

Chas thought, *How could they not believe in this when it is in the Bible?* He soon discovered that there were two groups of

Christians: charismatic and non-charismatic. This church intentionally puts out the Spirit's fire by not accepting the gifts and operating in them.

Paul warned church leaders not to do this: *"Therefore, my brothers, be eager to prophesy, and do not forbid speaking in tongues"* (1 Corinthians 14:39). Church leaders can make all the excuses in the world, but if they forbid prophesies and tongues in the church, they have disobeyed God, and worse, they have stopped God from helping His people.

This is an example of a question I'm asked on a consistent basis: "Brother Tom, if miracles are real, why haven't I seen any?" The answer is so simple: that person goes to a church that quenches the Spirit's fire. If a church does not want to see supernatural manifestations, then they will not see it. Many have stopped the work of the Holy Spirit.

Fear of the Supernatural

There is a tendency of human nature to avoid things that are mysterious or beyond rational explanation. And there is no rational explanation of the spiritual gifts. Let's be honest: many people are very uneasy when they witness a manifestation of the gifts. Think about the first time you heard someone speaking in tongues. How did you feel? Probably, at the very least, uncomfortable. Now remember the first time you saw demons manifested through someone. That probably made you afraid.

This is very much what happened to the people in Jesus' day. After Jesus delivered the demoniac in Gerasenes, the Bible says, *"Then all the people of the region of the Gerasenes asked Jesus to leave them, because they were overcome with fear. So he got into the boat and left"* (Luke 8:37).

Jesus accommodated them. He left. There was no point in His trying to bring a good thing to them if they were afraid of it.

The same thing happens today. If you are afraid of the gifts of the Spirit, the Lord will accommodate your fears and leave you alone. He will not push them on you if you are afraid.

This was not the only biblical instance in which people were afraid of the supernatural. The disciples were afraid when they saw Jesus walk on water and calm a storm. It is quite human to be afraid of what you cannot explain.

Holy Desire

Follow the way of love and eagerly desire spiritual gifts, especially the gift of prophecy. (1 Corinthians 14:1)

I suppose the best way to fan into flame the gift of God is to desire the gifts. Without holy desire, you are unlikely to see the gifts manifest in your life.

The first step to desiring the spiritual gifts is to experience them firsthand in your life. When I was an adolescent, my uncle married a Mexican woman who had a son named Gilbert. I was excited because I had a new cousin around my age to play with. Being from Mexico, Gilbert was not accustomed to American food, so when our family ordered pizza and offered some to Gilbert, he refused it.

He said, "I don't like pizza."

Wow! I had never heard of anyone who disliked pizza, so I asked, "Gilbert, when was the last time you ate pizza?"

He paused. "Uh, I actually haven't had any pizza before."

"How do you know you don't like it if you haven't tried it?" I begged him to eat it, but for months, he refused pizza when we had it at our house.

Finally, he reluctantly tried it. "Oh, wow!" Gilbert smiled. "This is good. I like it." Then he ate all our shares. To this day,

Gilbert loves pizza, but at first, he had thought he didn't. This reminds me of Psalm 34:8: *"Taste and see that the LORD is good."*

Some of you reading this book may have never experienced the gifts of the Spirit firsthand in your life, so you think you would not like them. You are like my cousin Gilbert. You will not know for sure whether you will like the gifts until you try using them. It has been my experience that when a Christian first experiences the gifts of the Spirit manifesting in their lives, they never want to be an ordinary Christian.

Let me take this food analogy one step further. Suppose it is against your religion to eat pork. When you smell bacon frying, you enjoy the aroma, but you will not eat it because you believe God forbids it. The same is true of those who have seen the gifts of the Spirit operate in other people's lives. They recognize the benefits of the spiritual gifts, but they have been taught that speaking in tongues is of the devil, or that healing and miracles are deceptions of Satan, or that prophecy is adding to the Bible. So they avoid them.

You might be one of those people. Be honest. You see the benefits. Accept them in your life; and when you experience them, you will understand how wonderful and beneficial they can be both in your life and in others'.

Finally, the way to create a holy desire for these gifts is to see them regularly in other people's lives. I know when I watch a minister operate in the gifts, I am filled with a desire to do the same. This is true of anything. You can create the desire by looking at it. Purposely follow ministries that regularly operate in the gifts of the Spirit. When you do, it will create in you the holy desire to move in the gifts; you will fan into flame the gift of God that is in you.

TWENTY-ONE

THE FRUIT OF THE SPIRIT

Smack in the middle of Paul's discourse on the gifts of the Spirit, he gives an important warning:

> If I speak in the tongues of men and of angels, but have not love, I am only a resounding gong or a clanging cymbal. If I have the gift of prophecy and can fathom all mysteries and all knowledge, and if I have a faith that can move mountains, but have not love, I am nothing. If I give all I possess to the poor and surrender my body to the flames, but have not love, I gain nothing.　　　　　　　　(1 Corinthians 13:1–3)

Paul reminds the believers that the Holy Spirit did not come only to give us gifts but that we would bear fruit, as well. And what better fruit does Paul mention than love? Although it is not the only fruit, love is the greatest fruit of all.

> But the fruit of the Spirit is love, joy, peace, patience, kindness, goodness, faithfulness, gentleness and self-control.
> 　　　　　　　　　　　　　　　(Galatians 5:22–23)

I find it interesting that Paul mentions nine fruits of the Spirit, which is the same number of gifts he mentions in 1 Corinthians 12:8–10.

Just as the high priests in the Old Testament wore a robe with an alternating pattern of bells and pomegranates affixed to the hem, so every gift of the Spirit has a corresponding fruit that we should bear.

A Better Person

In concluding this book, I felt it was important to remind you that the gifts can make you stronger and smarter, but only the fruit of the Spirit can make you a better person. Who could disagree with the beauty of these nine fruits? If you express love, joy, and peace, would that not make you a better person? Sure it would! How about showing patience and kindness to others; wouldn't that make you better? Would people consider you a good person if you lived a good and faithful life? Of course, they would. And if you were gentle with others and exercised self-control in your life, do you think your life would be better? There is no doubt that the fruits of the Spirit make you a better human being.

Satan's ultimate goal is to bring you into sin; but the fruits of the Spirit enable you to resist Satan more effectively.

The same Holy Spirit that gives you the gifts is the same Spirit that bears this fruit. He is the Giver of gifts and the Bearer of fruits. The difference between gifts and fruits is this: gifts are received, but fruit must be cultivated. And it is easier to receive a gift than it is to develop fruit. Yet the same Holy Spirit can help us develop the fruit in our lives.

The World Needs Help

While it is easy to know the meaning of the fruits, it is much harder to live them out. Consider these facts: prisons are filled to overflowing because of hate, greed, and lust. War and crime speak of the failure of mankind to maintain peace and gentleness.

Satan is responsible for war and crime, but the fruit of the Spirit can prevent these catastrophes. There is an old saying that goes, "An apple a day keeps the doctor away." This adage is meant to convey that if we eat fruit every day, we will not get sick. Society is very sick, and the only medicine that can cure it is the fruit of the Spirit.

Consider marriage. Two people fall in love and get married and are called to love their spouse for the rest of their lives. Yet half of marriages end in divorce. How could this happen if all couples, at some point, loved each other? It's simple: everyone needs help in loving. Love is difficult to express on our own; selfishness and resentment take the place of marital love.

Also consider the relationship of parents with children. Is there any greater love than what parents have for their own children? Yet many do not even talk to their kids. Even the strongest relationships have been strained.

If we have difficulty loving our spouses, children, and parents, how can we expect to love our neighbors, strangers, and enemies? Why do we expect nations to get along with each other when we have difficulty getting along with our own relatives and friends?

This is the failure of the human race to acknowledge that we need help to cultivate moral attributes that (I'm sure all of us could agree) make us better people. While people can show some fruit, it is obvious that, on their own, they lack the power to bear them in abundance.

The Church Needs Help

Jesus said, *"I am the vine; you are the branches. If a man remains in me and I in him, he will bear much fruit; apart from me you can do nothing"* (John 15:5). As much as we all would like to bear much fruit, we cannot do it without Christ. Jesus told us that we need

His help, and He has prayed to the Father, asking Him to send us another helper. The Helper is the Spirit.

Not only is it clear that, as a whole, the world has failed to live out the ideals of these nine moral attributes, but Christians themselves have often failed. It is because they have not relied on the help of the Spirit to cultivate the lovely fruit.

Churches lack unity, divided over selfish motives, doctrine, and ill-perceived offenses. Ministries struggle to make ends meet because of the disobedience and failure of their members to adhere to biblical principles. Congregations refuse to work with other churches for the common good because of fear, pride, and legalism.

Has it not become clear that we need the Holy Spirit to help us live how God calls us to live? We receive the help we need when we are baptized in the Spirit; then we must let Him cultivate the fruit of the Spirit within us.

The Law of Sin and Death

Paul described his frustrating life without the Spirit, saying, "For I have the desire to do what is good, but I cannot carry it out" (Romans 7:18). It was not about a lack of desire to be holy but a lack of ability. He didn't say, "I will not carry it out," but *"I cannot carry it out."* He just could not! This is our state without the Spirit.

Paul continued, *"For what I do is not the good I want to do; no, the evil I do not want to do—this I keep on doing"* (verse 19). Does this seem like your experience, as well?

You tried giving up cigarettes—you really wanted to quit—but you felt too weak and went back to them again. You told yourself that you would be more patient with your children, but when they did it again, you lost it. You screamed and yelled just as you had done before. You made a commitment to live a joyful life and refused to give into depression. But despite your resolve, you sunk deeper into depression.

It's not about willpower or resolve or holy desire; it's about power. You are powerless; without Jesus Christ, *"you can do nothing"* (John 15:5).

Paul then gave the answer to his dilemma and the dilemma of every believer: *"Through Christ Jesus the law of the Spirit of life set me free from the law of sin and death"* (Romans 8:2). Paul described his bondage to the *"law of sin and death"* and his freedom by the *"law of the Spirit of life."* The Holy Spirit supersedes the law of sin and death.

In physics, a law is a constant controlling force, such as gravity. Let's imagine for a moment that I decided I was going to lift up my Bible high in the air as a symbol of my desire to live by the laws of God. How long would I be able to hold it above my head? For a couple of minutes…maybe even longer. But, eventually, I would get tired and have to lay it down. It wouldn't be from a lack of desire; it would be because I was physically tired. I just wouldn't have the natural power to do this.

Paul calls sin a law. Like gravity, sin is constantly pulling us down when we try to do right. While I may be able to do right for a while, eventually sin—a law—will tire me out, so that I will eventually give up and sin. This is the experience of every human being, including Christians.

Paul's answer is the Spirit. The Holy Spirit, who is also a law, is a constant controlling force in our lives. He is stronger than sin. He can outlast sin in our lives.

For example, I do not have any natural ability to fly a plane, but I can get on an airplane and let the pilot do the work. I can nap, eat, and rest while the pilot flies the plane. The plane exerts a force over gravity. While gravity is still working, the force of "lift" supersedes the force of gravity.

So it is with us when it comes to becoming a better person. While I can occasionally be good on my own, eventually I will get exhausted and succumb to temptation. I may look at a person with lust, or be overly harsh with someone who needs my compassion, or worry over a situation that I should put in God's care. So how can I become better? Not by my willpower or resolve. The world depends on willpower or resolve to change us; but God has a better solution. He sent us His Holy Spirit to help us. Through the Spirit in our lives, we can do remarkable acts of kindness. We can forgive the worse offenses and resist the strongest temptation. It is not because we have some innate ability to do it but because there is Someone in us who gives us the ability.

Pour Love in Our Hearts

Years ago, I worked for a businessman named Joseph who was very hard to get along with. The employees hated him, and I, too, disliked him at first. He picked fights with the customers and constantly scolded the employees.

At this time, I was just learning about the Holy Spirit. I read Romans 5:5, "*God has poured out his love into our hearts by the Holy Spirit, whom he has given us,*" and told the Lord, "There is no way I could ever love this man on my own; but with the Holy Spirit pouring love in my heart for him, I could." I asked the Lord for this great love, and I began to say out loud, "I have love for Joseph, because God has poured out His love into my heart by the Holy Spirit."

From that time on, I had a supernatural ability to love Joseph. The employees were asking me how I could stand the man and treat him so kindly and not get upset when he lost his temper. I told them, "The Holy Spirit has given me this love." I smiled at

Joseph and never allowed his temper and rude remarks to affect me. After a while, Joseph's attitude toward me changed. He actually began to like me. At a special banquet dinner, while others avoided Joseph, I went up to him and talked to him as if he were my buddy. After the dinner, one of the employees said, "I can't believe you got along with Joseph." Again, I told them that it was the Holy Spirit.

I have learned that on my own I cannot love people like Joseph, and neither can you; but with the Holy Spirit pouring His love into our hearts, supernaturally we can love. This is what we need right now: a baptism of love. The baptism in the Holy Spirit gives us additional love that we do not have on our own. In addition to pouring out love into our hearts, He pours out every good quality we need to live better lives: joy, peace, patience, kindness, goodness, faithfulness, gentleness, and self-control.

If you lack any of these fruits in your life, simply admit to God you need help. Ask the Holy Spirit to help you. Claim out loud that all the fruits have been given to you—"I have joy, peace and patience"—and you will discover a supernatural ability to cultivate these and all the other fruits of the Spirit.

Prune the Branch

> *I am the true vine, and my Father is the gardener. He cuts off every branch in me that bears no fruit, while every branch that does bear fruit he prunes so that it will be even more fruitful. You are already clean because of the word I have spoken to you.* (John 15:1–3)

One last thing we need to do in order to cultivate the fruit of the Spirit is to listen to the Word of God that the Holy Spirit inspired men to write. When we read Scripture and hear them explained to us, we are being pruned. A pruned branch actually helps a tree grow more fruit. At first, cutting off unfruitful stems seems to make a tree more barren. Yet it is essential for a gardener to prune dead branches that bear no fruit so that they do not take up nutrients. In this way, the nutrients can get to the healthy branches to make them more fruitful.

For example, if you are not producing the fruit of love, then you need to read Scriptures about love and hear sermons about the love. As you do, the Word convicts you of the changes you need to make. And as you submit yourself to the Word you read or hear, the fruit of the Spirit will enter into your life. This is why the preaching of the Word of God is vital—it prunes us!

The same process can be applied to any of the nine fruits of the Spirit. If you lack joy, then read Scriptures on joy and listen to messages on joy. The same goes for if you lack peace or anything else. You need to focus on the parts of the Word that talk about the fruits you lack. When your body lacks certain nutrients, you will begin to crave certain foods with those nutrients. It is your body's way of getting the nutrients it needs. In the same way, if you lack a spiritual fruit, begin to feed yourself with the Word of God.

Don't avoid the parts of the Word that you don't like, especially those that chastise you. Otherwise you will lack the necessary pruning to be fruitful. But as you submit to the whole Word of God, you will be pruned and the fruit of the Spirit will be abundant and active in your life. You will be a better person.

Satan Fears You

As you learn about your spiritual gifts for spiritual warfare, Satan will fear you. You have weapons and fruit that you can use against him. When he tries to tell you a lie, you have wisdom and knowledge. When he afflicts you with sickness, you have the gift of healing. When he attempts to deceive you, you have the discerning of spirits. When he tries to corrupt your morality, you have the fruit of the Spirit. It is now time to walk in the Spirit. Operate the gifts; live the fruits. These are your weapons against Satan.

AFTERWORD

HAVE THE GIFTS PASSED AWAY?

One of Satan's top lies that he has propagated through the church is that the gifts of the Spirit have disappeared. Satan would love for you to believe this because it would leave you with fewer weapons to use against him. The truth is, every gift of the Spirit that was given to the early church is available to us today. Satan will actually distort the Bible in an attempt to prove that God removed some of the gifts for us today. This should not surprise us, because Satan twisted the Bible to try to get Jesus to jump off the pinnacle of the temple. The devil knows the Bible, but he distorts it for his advantage. He has done this through ministers of the gospel. He has convinced millions of Christians that the gifts of the Spirit have passed away. Let us look carefully at how Satan has crafted this lie. Here is a Scripture passage he has perverted to make believers think that some gifts of the Spirit have passed away:

> Love never fails. But where there are prophecies, they will cease; where there are tongues, they will be stilled; where there is knowledge, it will pass away. For we know in part and we prophesy in part, but when perfection comes, the imperfect disappears. When I was a child, I talked like a child, I thought

> *like a child, I reasoned like a child. When I became a man, I put childish ways behind me. Now we see but a poor reflection as in a mirror; then we shall see face to face. Now I know in part; then I shall know fully, even as I am fully known.*
>
> (1 Corinthians 13:8–12)

The gifts will end at the dawn of the new age of Christ's reign. But Satan lies by using this passage to say that the gifts ended *before* the new age.

There will be a time when we do not need the gifts of the Spirit, such as prophecy or words of knowledge or tongues. We will not need the gift of mountain-moving faith in the new age when death is swallowed up in victory. But for now, we live in a world of darkness where the light of knowledge is needed. We live in a world of demons and deception in which the discerning of Spirits is essential. We live in a world wracked in pain and disease where the gift of healing is wanted. We still do not know what to pray at all times, so we rely on the gift of tongues to pray when we are unsure of what God's will is.

Some Christians will say that the reason they cannot heal the sick anymore is because the gifts of healing have passed away. Who told them that? Not God! The reason some people have not been able to heal the sick is not because God took the gift away but because Satan has convinced them that God took it away. Listen, there is nothing in Scripture or history to even come close to teaching that the gifts of the Spirit have ended.

When Did the Gifts Disappear?

If God took those gifts away, then when did He do it? What Scripture tells us the date on which God would remove the gifts? And what took place in the world that made the gifts no longer necessary? People still get sick, so the gifts of healing are still necessary. The same could be said of every other gift of the Spirit.

There is nothing that has taken place in the world that makes any of the gifts obsolete. Certainly, when the new world comes, there will be no sickness and therefore no need for healing. This is true for every gift of the Spirit. There will be no need for any of the gifts at that time, because in the new world, everything will undergo a fundamental change from disorder to order; from ignorance to knowledge; from doubt to faith. In short, as long as we live in this imperfect world, we need the spiritual weapons.

Speculation on When the Gifts Disappeared

There are a lot of people who believe that the gifts of the Spirit have disappeared; but among them are differing beliefs on when it happened.

1. The Gifts Disappeared When the Last Apostle Died.

Some teach that the gifts ended when the last apostle died. But why would the death of an apostle cause the gifts to end? They argue that only the apostles had the gifts of the Spirit. But the Scriptures tell us that many who were not apostles also had the gifts of the Spirit. For examples, Philip the Evangelist cast out demons and healed the sick (see Acts 8:4–8) and the sick are instructed to approach their church elders to be anointed and healed (see James 5:14).

Paul wrote, *"Now to each one the manifestation of the Spirit is given for the common good"* (1 Corinthians 12:7). Gifts were not given only to the apostles but to *"each one,"* or to each believer. Many people are given the gift of healing.

2. The Gifts Disappeared When the Bible Was Completed.

There is another group that says that the gifts disappeared when the Bible was completed. So, presumably, when John penned the last words in the book of Revelation, the last book of the Bible, God took away His gifts. Is that what happened? What historical or biblical proof is offered for this? It is pure speculation.

3. The Gifts Disappeared When the Bible Was Canonized.

Finally, others hold to the theory that the gifts ended when the Bible was canonized. So it's not the Word of God that claims the gifts have ended but the council of bishops who decided which books really constituted the Word of God. The belief that the act of canonization of the Bible ended the gifts is ludicrous.

As you can see, not even those who say that the gifts of the Spirit have passed away are in agreement on when it happened. There are at least three different views. Yet none of them are supported by either Scripture or history. There is not one writing from the ancient fathers that says the gifts ended when the last apostle died; there are no plausible writings or treatises confirming that the gifts ended when the Word of God was completed or when the bishops canonized the Bible. Did God, like a vacuum cleaner, suck up all the gifts of the Spirit when the books of the Bible were finalized? No. God did not teach that the gifts ended; the church fathers did not teach that the gifts ended; Satan is the one who taught this. He is afraid of the gifts of the Spirit, so he wants us to believe that some of the gifts, our weapons of warfare, are not available anymore.

History of the Gifts

We have ample evidence in the writings of the church fathers that the gifts of the Spirit were still present in the church after all the apostles had died. In 150 AD, Justin Martyr wrote to a Jewish skeptic Trophis, "Now, it is possible to see amongst us women and men who possess gifts of the Spirit of God....For the prophetical gifts remain with us, even to this present time."

Irenaeus, near the end of the second century, wrote, "In like manner do we also hear many brethren in the church who possess prophetic gifts, and who through the Spirit speak all kinds of languages."

We also have accounts of the gifts of the Spirit continuing after the canonization of the Bible. Augustine, who was the first to suggest that the gifts disappeared, later changed his mind when the gifts were rekindled in the church. He wrote, "We still do what the apostles did when they laid hands on the Samaritans and called down the Holy Spirit on them in the laying-on of hands. It is expected that converts should speak with new tongues." These words came in 400 AD, after the Bible was canonized.

As you can see, there is no historical or experiential proof that speaking in tongues has disappeared. Today, hundreds of millions of Christians have the gifts of the Spirit. Many have displayed the gift of speaking in tongues, gifts of prophecy, and so forth. How, then, can one argue that it has disappeared?

Behind in No Spiritual Gift

It is disappointing that people have allowed Satan to twist Paul's words in 1 Corinthians 13 to teach that the gifts disappeared. However, this erroneous teaching ignores the first chapter of this epistle. In it, Paul clearly teaches that the gifts of the Spirit would remain until Christ returns. Look at what he wrote: *"Therefore you do not lack **any spiritual gift** as you eagerly wait for our Lord Jesus Christ to be revealed"* (1 Corinthians 1:7). Notice that Paul said the church would *"not lack any spiritual gift"* until a certain event takes place. What event? When the Lord Jesus Christ is revealed. This is a clear reference to the coming of Jesus from heaven. Paul also said, *"This will happen when the Lord Jesus is revealed from heaven"*

(2 Thessalonians 1:7). Paul is saying that none of the gifts will disappear until Jesus comes back from heaven.

When Christ returns and perfects the world, the gifts of the Spirit will no longer be necessary. There will be no ignorance, sickness, demons, difficulties, and anything bad that requires the Holy Spirit's gifts.

Paul believed that all the spiritual gifts would remain until Jesus Christ returns. So, until then, let us seek earnestly the gifts of the Spirit. Don't let Satan convince you that the gifts of the Spirit have ended.

ABOUT THE AUTHOR

Tom Brown is best known for his deliverance ministry. Millions have seen him on ABC's *20/20*, as well as on MSNBC and the History Channel. He is a noted conference speaker, prolific author, and committed pastor. His award-winning Internet site, www.tbm.org, reaches more than a million people each year. His previous books include *You Can Predict Your Future*; *Devil, Demons, and Spiritual Warfare*; *Breaking Curses, Experiencing Healing*; and *Prayers That Get Results*. Tom resides in El Paso, Texas, with his beautiful wife, Sonia. They have three children together and are empty nesters.

Welcome to Our House!

We Have a Special Gift for You

It is our privilege and pleasure to share in your love of Christian books. We are committed to bringing you authors and books that feed, challenge, and enrich your faith.

To show our appreciation, we invite you to sign up to receive a specially selected **Reader Appreciation Gift**, with our compliments. Just go to the Web address at the bottom of this page.

God bless you as you seek a deeper walk with Him!

WE HAVE A GIFT FOR YOU. VISIT:

whpub.me/nonfictionthx

WHITAKER HOUSE